Praise for *Never Can Say Goodbye*

"*Never Can Say Goodbye* is deliciously woven from threads of guidance, memory, and devotion to the sacred labor of holding space at the end of life. With clear-eyed tenderness and his signature storyteller's grace, Darnell Lamont Walker makes the complex, often unseen work of the death doula accessible and deeply human. Through quiet moments and honest reflections, he offers not just insight, but presence—a reminder that death, too, deserves care, clarity, and compassion."

—Alua Arthur, author of *Briefly Perfectly Human*

"This master storyteller shares the lessons of loss that have found their way into his heart (and now these pages), offering us a captivating and wise guide to a good life and a good death. Anyone who seeks a rich life and accepts that we will all die should read *Never Can Say Goodbye*."

—Dale G. Larson, PhD, J. Thomas and Kathleen L. McCarthy Professor, Counseling Psychology, Santa Clara University, and author of *The Helper's Journey: Empathy, Compassion and the Challenge of Caring*

"Darnell Lamont Walker is a storyteller for the ages, weaving threads of life and death into a tapestry that reminds us of the beauty that's possible in our endings. *Never Can Say*

Goodbye is the field guide for the walk we will all take, the must-have death resource for every human."

—Helen Bauer, BSN, RN, CHPN, end-of-life educator and advocate, host of *The Heart of Hospice* podcast, and owner of Hospice Navigation Services

"*Never Can Say Goodbye* should be required reading for every single human being. With poetic precision and radical tenderness, Darnell Lamont Walker invites us into a sacred threshold where love and loss meet. This is a guidebook for the heart. Darnell doesn't just write about death. He reminds us how to live—more presently, more courageously, and more connected than ever before. This is the kind of book that becomes a companion for life."

—Justin Michael Williams, Grammy-nominated artist and author of *Stay Woke*

"A profoundly engaging and inspiring exploration of what it means to hold space and accompany people at the end of their lives. These stories are tender, inspiring, and sometimes sprinkled with humor, always inviting us to show up compassionately with our full humanity for people facing the hardest days of their lives."

—Lisa Keefauver, author of *Grief Is a Sneaky Bitch*

"*Never Can Say Goodbye* is a loving and gentle reminder that as long as we're breathing, we still have time to live our lives in the ways we've always wanted, making even the smallest pieces of our dreams come true, and creating something even better than what we'd imagined."

—Lisa Deaderick, columnist for *The San Diego Union-Tribune*

"*Never Can Say Goodbye* is a tender, unflinching exploration of how we love each other through death. With reverence, wit, and a wide-open heart, Darnell Lamont Walker brings us into sacred rooms, hospital bedsides, kitchen tables, and quiet gravesides, and he tells us how to show up. This book not only honors the universal truths of grief but also beautifully centers the often-overlooked stories of families of color and Black men grieving with grace and complexity. Darnell doesn't just teach us how to die well—he teaches us how to live more meaningfully in the face of mortality."

—Claire Bidwell Smith, author of *Conscious Grieving and Anxiety: The Missing Stage of Grief*

"*Never Can Say Goodbye* takes the reader on an intimate journey into the world of a death doula. With tenderness and reverence, Walker captures the powerful moments that unfold within death, dying, and grief, writing with a vulnerability that cracks the reader open and a sacredness that lingers far after finishing this book. This book will move you, inspire you, and have you sharing it with everyone you know."

—Lisa Pahl, founder of The Death Deck

"In *Never Can Say Goodbye,* Darnell Lamont Walker assembles a cast of characters that could be easily you or me. Providing snapshots of their interactions with death while living or being no more, we catch glimpses of what it means to be human on the verge of transition and human bearing witness to that process."

—Kwame Otu, professor and author of *Amphibious Subjects*

"Darnell Lamont Walker has weaved words into a spiritual portrait to teach us how to embrace death by living our lives so meaningfully that we will never die. As you sit and cuddle with *Never Can Say Goodbye,* I hope you find yourself prepared and unafraid of the death that awaits us. *Never Can Say Goodbye* encourages you to release any fears associated with thoughts of death, write a love letter (obituary) to yourself, prepare, and get about the business of living."

—Nikuyah Walker, former mayor of Charlottesville, Virginia

NEVER CAN SAY GOODBYE

The Life of a Death Doula and the Art of a Peaceful End

Darnell Lamont Walker

HARPERONE
An Imprint of HarperCollins*Publishers*

This is a work of nonfiction. The events and experiences detailed herein are all true and have been faithfully rendered to the best of the author's abilities. Some names, identifying features, and circumstances have been changed in order to protect the anonymity of the various individuals involved. The goal in these instances is to protect people's privacy without damaging the integrity of the story.

 For information, address HarperCollins Publishers, 195 Broadway, New York, NY 10007. In Europe, HarperCollins Publishers, Macken House, 39/40 Mayor Street Upper, Dublin 1, D01 C9W8, Ireland.

HarperCollins books may be purchased for educational, business, or sales promotional use. For information, please email the Special Markets Department at SPsales@harpercollins.com.

harpercollins.com

FIRST EDITION

Designed by Jason Kayser
Author photograph on page 261 copyright © Kristen Finn

Library of Congress Cataloging-in-Publication Data has been applied for.

ISBN 978-0-06-342183-7

25 26 27 28 29 LBC 5 4 3 2 1

For those who held it together when they needed to fall apart. For the ones who carried the weight of others' grief while theirs went unseen.

Contents

NEVER
CAN
SAY
GOODBYE

Prologue

BEFORE WE BEGIN, I WANT TO THANK YOU FOR OPENING this book. Whether it landed in your hands by chance or you sought it out, I believe you're here for a reason. You feel it, too, that's why you're still reading. Maybe you're curious about what a death doula does, maybe you're facing your own mortality—aren't we all? Or maybe you're walking with someone at the end of their life, or feel you might soon. Wherever you are, I hope this book not only meets you in that place but also helps to make that place softer, lighter, and if not now, eventually a place where joy exists, too.

As you read, I want you to feel the emotions. The stories are tender and raw, and they may stir something deep in you. Take your time. Let the words sit with you. Grief, love, and the full spectrum of emotions deserve to be held, not rushed. If you need to pause, cry, or simply breathe, know that's okay. These pages aren't meant to be powered through; they're an invitation to sit with life's hardest truths and find meaning in the weight they carry. Let yourself move at a pace that feels right for you.

I'd like to start by telling you a story about a nine-year-old boy who didn't know the journey he was beginning when his grandmother pulled him into conversations about death and dying. That little boy was me, and my grandmother, Irene Elizabeth Jones, was a woman who understood life and death in ways I wouldn't fully appreciate until much later—perhaps not until she was at the end of her life and I was the one walking her home. It all started with her sister, Greta Mae. Greta Mae was dying, though at the time, I had such a limited understanding of what that really meant. What I did know was that my grandmother sat with me, and we talked. We talked about life, how to love people when they're suffering, and what it means to be there for someone when they're leaving this world. We talked, I suspect now, because no one else in the family wanted anything to do with discussions about death, and I was there, always like her shadow, listening to everything she said. She'd been to the hospital every day to visit, to care for her sister, to love her, to talk with her and listen. My grandmother never named her actions as "being a death doula," and I didn't realize that the conversations in her living room were the beginning of the path I'm now inviting you to walk with me.

I want you to picture this for a moment: two people, one older and one young, sitting together in a quiet room awakening to the sounds of griping men out front and children playing red light, green light out back. The sounds halt when the older one speaks, not because the world fell silent but because to the younger one, the older one's voice is everything. My grandmother had this way of making the world feel smaller, like everything outside could wait and all that mattered was the present. She spoke to me in her calm, steady voice, telling me stories about her life with her sister, about the things Greta Mae loved and the life she lived. There was no fear in her words, no hesitation in talking about the fact that Greta Mae was dying. My grandmother didn't shy away from death, and because of her, neither did I. She showed me that death wasn't something to be afraid of but something to prepare for, something that could even be beautiful if we approached it with love.

At nine years old, I didn't have the language to understand what was happening, but I felt the weight of it. I didn't know then that those conversations were laying the foundation for the work I do now as a death doula. But that's the thing about life, isn't it? Sometimes we don't realize we've started a journey until we look back and see how all the pieces fit together on the trail behind us.

So what is a death doula? Simply put, a death doula is someone who accompanies a person through the dying process. We hold space for them, listen to their stories, and help them make choices that honor the way they want to leave this life. But there's so much more to it than that. It's not just about the logistics of death, though those are important; it's about the emotional, spiritual, and relational aspects, too. It's about being there when someone is scared, when they need someone to talk to in the middle of the night, when they want to tell the story of their life one last time.

Being a death doula means understanding that death is as much a part of life as walking for the first time, saying our first words, having that first kiss; as much a part of life as birth. It's about realizing that, in the end, what people want most is to be seen, heard, and loved. They want to know that their life mattered, that their story will be remembered. And it's my job to help them feel that, to help them find peace in those final days, hours, and moments.

But here's the thing I want you to know: You've probably already done some of this work yourself. You might not call yourself a death doula, but if you've ever sat with someone who was grieving, if you've ever listened to a loved one tell a story from their past, if you've ever been there for someone when they needed comfort—you've already been doing the work. You've been holding space, just like my grandmother held space for me all those years ago.

I was a death doula long before I knew what a death doula was. Funny thing is, I didn't need to know the name to understand the work, and I suspect the same could be said for my grandmother. She never heard the term "death doula" either, but she lived it. And so did her mother, if the stories passed down the line are to be trusted. This legacy runs deeper than any title.

Take Yvette, for example. When she called me, it wasn't to help her face death. No, she wanted help telling her story—the one she'd leave behind for "the brave folk ready to really know me." She didn't care to talk about the heart condition that was speeding up her departure, and I respected that. Neither of us knew that week would be her last. Her daughter, Tasha, opened the door when I arrived, her eyes red-rimmed, already exhausted. She hugged me, thanking me for coming, then immediately said, "I'm not ready to lose her."

There's always this question lingering in the room that rarely gets said aloud: "What do we do and say when we know there's not much time left?" I didn't need to ask Tasha; she showed me. While I sat with Yvette, taking notes on the life she lived—oh, the things that woman had seen—Tasha was there, quietly at her mother's side, stroking her hair like she was memorizing its feel, breathing in the star jasmine coming through the window and the lavender scent coming from Yvette's hands every time she moisturized them. Tasha clipped her mother's nails and rubbed lotion into her feet. She filled in the blanks when Yvette got lost in a story. Tasha knew all the details—the exact angle of sunlight coming through the windshield on that road trip they took to Big Sur, and the way Yvette laughed when she recounted burning the Christmas turkey.

One afternoon, while Yvette slept, I turned to Tasha and said, "You know, you should think about being a death doula." She looked at me like I'd lost my mind. "I could never do that," she said, shaking her head. "I'm not nearly strong enough."

I wondered if she realized what she'd been doing all week. "You're helping someone transition right now," I told her, watching the realization cross her face. "You're here making all the difference in her final moments." And it was true. Tasha was there, showing up for her mother in ways that mattered. That's what a death doula does.

I've never taken this work lightly, and I'll never sugarcoat the challenges it brings. For those who think it's reserved for the especially strong or trained, I always ask them to think about the times they've been there for someone at the end. Maybe it was a parent, a friend, or even someone they didn't know that well. You don't need to be extraordinary to be there in those moments. You just need to show up.

David, for instance, called me when his best friend, Scotty, was nearing the end. They had been inseparable since childhood, and David didn't know how to prepare for losing that connection. He'd show up at Scotty's place after work every day, soup in hand, though Scotty rarely touched it. His appetite was already gone by the time I got there. But David never failed to bring the things that made Scotty smile—hot fries, weed edibles they would giggle over, old stories about their wild years. Scotty loved the edibles. He didn't love talking about dying, not when it was taking pieces of him so fast, but David was always ready, tears hanging in the corners of his eyes, asking, "What can I do for you now?"

One day, Scotty let me in on what he hoped for when his time came. He wanted to be flooded with all the good moments, the beautiful things he'd seen and done. He said he wanted them to hit him like "a love running through tall grass."

I can still hear him saying that. There was a beach in Curaçao he wished he could swim to again, but he'd settle for seeing it one last time in his mind. And he wanted to remember the face of a boy he fell for as a teenager, the taste of the pound cake he used to make with his grandma. He was halfway through telling me about hearing Sade's "Cherish the Day" for the first time when he stopped, looked over, and said, "Make sure David knows how much this means to me." So, the next morning, I did. I told David what his presence meant to Scotty while he could still hear it and see the gratitude in his friend's eyes. I think of David often because he would tell me, over and over, that he couldn't imagine doing what I do. When Scotty passed, I reminded David that he did exactly what he thought he couldn't—he just showed up for his friend, and he did it beautifully.

And then there's Lisa. Her husband, James, was diagnosed with ALS, and it took over his body faster than any of us expected. Lisa quit her job, became his full-time caregiver, and poured her whole self into making sure he had the ending he wanted. She called me for respite, but sometimes—most times—she wouldn't leave. She couldn't tear herself away, even when she was exhausted. The love she had for James was so woven into her care for him, you couldn't separate the two. Lisa woke from a nap on the cot next to James's bed, looked over to me and said, "I could never do what you do." I waved my hand, playfully dismissing her, and let her know I watched her do exactly what I do, and more.

So you see, this book isn't just about what I've done or what a death doula is. It's about helping you see that you, too, have the capacity to love others in their most vulnerable moments. It's about showing you how to hold space for someone who is dying, how to help them feel seen and heard, and how to honor their wishes in their final days. It's about recognizing that death is not something to fear but something to face with love, courage, and as my dear friend Alua Arthur says, grace.

I remember the first time I sat with someone who was at the end of their life. I had been called in by the family to sit with a woman who was dying. Her body was frail, her breath shallow, but her eyes were full of life. We didn't talk much—sometimes, there's nothing that needs to be said—but I sat with her, held her hand, and listened to the rhythm of her breathing. In those moments I felt the weight of what it means to be human. I wasn't just witnessing the end of a life; I was witnessing the culmination of all the stories she had lived, the love she had given, and the legacy she would leave behind.

That's what being a death doula is about. It's about being present, not just physically but also emotionally and spiritually. It's about creating a space where someone can be vulnerable, where they can express their fears, hopes, and regrets. It's about helping them tell their story in whatever way they choose, whether that's through words, silence, or the presence of those they love.

My grandmother understood this intuitively. When Greta Mae was dying, my grandmother didn't fill the room with chatter or distraction. She let the silence settle in, let it become a companion rather than something to be avoided. And she showed others how to do the same. She understood that sometimes the greatest gift you can give someone is your presence, your willingness to sit with them in their pain and not try to fix it. I'm grateful she let me watch her do this over and over again for friends and family.

As I've walked this path as a death doula, I've realized that I don't have all the answers, and I can't take away the pain or the fear that comes with dying. I can be there. I can listen. I can help those ready to face their mortality tell their story in whatever way they need to tell it.

Be present. Be love.

When I was twelve, my cousin Maine came back home to Virginia to die. He was older than me, but I remember feeling this sense of responsibility—almost like I was stepping into something bigger than myself. My grandmother and I took care of him together, and without even realizing it, I began to apply everything she'd been teaching me over the years. All those quiet lessons she'd woven into our conversations about death and love, about sitting with people in their final moments, came rushing back. We didn't have a formal plan, but it was like we both knew exactly what needed to be done. She cooked and I told jokes. I'd hang his clothes on the line and she'd catch him up on the family drama. We hugged him and ate with him and listened to him. And when I'd forget, my grandmother showed me how to care for him with the same tenderness she'd shown me when she first started talking to me about death. She knew this wasn't just about providing physical care—it was about emotional care, too. Maine's body may have been failing, but his spirit needed to feel loved and seen, and that's what we focused on.

A year later, when I was thirteen, I found myself volunteering at a hospice and care home after school, not realizing then, of course, how much of what I'd learned there would pour out into the lives of others and into this book. My friends were all old enough to work with a permit, but I wasn't, and I needed something to fill my time after school. I ended up connecting with so many of the people being cared for and their families as well. Of course, these weren't formal sessions or structured visits; I was just an activities coordinator. Sometimes we'd play games or talk, and other times we'd just sit in silence. Again, looking back, I now see those pieces fill in the path.

There's something sacred about being with someone at the end of their life. It's like standing at the edge of the ocean, being pulled in and out by the tide, knowing that something larger than yourself is at work. It's humbling, beautiful, and heartbreaking all at once—as are so many of the stories in this book. When I think back to those early conversations in that living room on Hardy Drive in Charlottesville, Virginia, with my grandmother, I realize that she was preparing me for this work long before I knew it. And perhaps what she didn't know—or maybe she did—is that she was preparing me to be the person she needed at the end of her life.

She was teaching me how to love people through the hardest moments of their lives. She was showing me that death isn't something to be feared but something to be met with compassion. And most of all, she was teaching me that every life has a story worth telling, a story that deserves to be heard.

Your story matters. I've been writing for over three decades now, and my journey as a writer has shaped much of how I approach my work as a death doula. These days, I write professionally for children, creating content that introduces them to parts of life where they can find joy, resilience, and a sense of wonder—much of what I hope my death doula clients find when I arrive, if they are able. My hope is to help children grow into adults who aren't paralyzed by fear of death or weighed down by the pressures of a joyless existence. Instead, I want to offer them the tools and perspectives that could help them embrace life fully—and eventually, when the time comes, death too. It's a delicate balance, but I believe that if we begin these conversations early, we can raise a generation of people who see death as a natural part of the cycle, not something to be feared or avoided.

As you continue, I want you to take a moment to consider your own capacity for love and presence. Each of us has the ability to touch lives, even in their final moments. Whether you're a friend, a family member, or even a stranger, your willingness to show up has and will mean far more than you can fathom, until it's your turn to be cared for at the end.

Allow yourself to reflect on the experiences that shaped

you, the moments of vulnerability that invited you to show up for others, and the lessons you've learned along the way. Embrace the idea that you can be a source of comfort and strength for those navigating the turbulent waters of grief and transition, while letting go of the idea that you have to show up a certain way. I hope this journey with me empowers you to embrace the inevitable changes life brings while also finding joy in the everyday moments.

Never Can Say Goodbye isn't just about dying—it's about living fully, loving deeply, and as the incomparable Sade sings about, cherishing the day. It's about finding light in the shadows and recognizing that even as we prepare to say goodbye, we're also celebrating the incredible threads of life that connect us all. I invite you to walk this path with me, to engage with the stories and insights shared, and to find your own voice in the conversations. Together we can cultivate a space where we not only honor the lives we've touched but also embrace the beauty of our shared humanity.

In many ways, this book is a love letter to my grandmother, to the lessons she taught me about life and death, and to the way she loved people so fully in their final moments. But it's also a love letter to you, dear reader, because I believe that you, too, have the capacity to love in this way. You, too, can hold space for someone else, just as my grandmother held space for so many, and just as I now hold space for others.

THE SOLDIER

ON A BATHROOM WALL IN A DC CAFÉ IN 2012, I READ George Eliot's words for the first time: "If we had a keen vision and feeling of all ordinary human life, it would be like hearing the grass grow and the squirrel's heartbeat, and we should die of that roar which lies on the other side of silence." Bathroom walls, I believe, have always been the place where true inspiration and true art are found. I understood those words deeply, and it began to make sense to me why the emotions, especially the grief, of others felt so personal. I can recount times when the grief of others felt very much like my own. When I began leaning into death work with intention, everyone was calling themselves an empath; I, being one to always steer clear of herds—having seen what happened to Mufasa—avoided it. George Eliot tells me it's a keen vision or maybe the power of a radical kind of empathy that unveils the hidden burdens and invisible grief many carry.

Funerals and whatever folks choose as their memorial service are the rites of passage that bid the final farewell to the dead. They are often solemn occasions, but I've known many to be beautifully loud celebrations where memories are shared to piece together the dead person's life. They are places where tears, like laughter, come in waves, and some silk-voiced songbird belts out one of those old-school gospel songs that sends the entire room into a trance. It's usually a rendition of Thomas Dorsey's "Precious Lord, Take My Hand," a song he's said to have written while mourning his wife and son, both who died in childbirth. But no matter how the life of the dead is honored on this occasion, amid the grief and remembrance, there too often exists a realm of untold stories concealed beneath the surface of formalities and rituals. Such was the case at the graveside celebration for Maurice, an eighty-year-old former marine, whose life story unfolded in layers of complexity and depth, revealing the unspoken truths of love and human connection.

One day before the memorial service, my godfather Herbert called to tell me he ran into a woman at a market in Charlottesville. Her name was Shelly and she sparked up a conversation and asked where she should eat and what she should see other than Thomas Jefferson's plantation home and the university he founded. Herbert is stylish, always in the latest fashions from cap to sole; and he's approachable, wearing a smile and kind eyes everywhere he goes, so this was no shocker. He asked what brought her to Charlottesville and learned she'd come for her cousin's memorial service the following day, prompting her to ask if he knew a photographer who could take photos. I was his first call. I was freshly home, having just returned to the States from wandering around Peru, Brazil, and Ecuador with nothing but a backpack and a large appetite, and immediately said yes, knowing this would at minimum be a story to share later about the time I snapped photos at the funeral of a stranger. At most, it'd be an opportunity to witness this death ceremony and be a system of support for anyone in attendance who needed it.

The next day, I arrived early to the cemetery with my fair-condition Canon camera and met Shelly under what she said was a bald cypress tree. I'm rarely nervous when meeting folks for the first time, but when death is involved, it changes things. How they will show up to the meeting is always the unknown. This isn't a date to that favorite restaurant, or a James Vincent McMorrow concert at sunset on a rooftop, or an art show with their favorite oil painter. It's a funeral, and the way my nerves are set up, I'm always on my way to the venue wondering which version of me I'll need to be to better support the grieving. However, beneath that tree, Shelly's inviting smile bloomed and embraced me, and I echoed its warmth with a greeting smile of my own. Shelly walked me to the graveside where seats and shades were set up for the few friends and one cousin in attendance. All of the attendees were as old as Maurice, and most of the men adorned their hats and jackets with military pins, stripes, and acronyms. Their wives wore the funeral dresses that I'm sure stayed ironed and ready in the closet for what one said was an almost weekly calendar item.

When I show up to spaces meant for death and dying as something other than a griever, a death doula, a speaker, or a comforting embrace in times of sadness, I have to remind myself to focus on the task at hand. Strangely, this has happened more times than I can count. I've been in death spaces as a poet, a maker of toast (the baked bread kind), and a makeshift puppeteer. At this graveside, as the photographer for Maurice's funeral and Shelly's memories, I embarked on a journey that transcended the mere documentation of moments. For whatever reason—and that reason probably being the universe saw fit to bring Shelly to Herbert, then to me—I was entrusted with the task of preserving memories beyond the confines of the present. What I hadn't considered at that time, but would soon discover, is that every person in the space is serving the process for the dead and the dying. I know now that even as the photographer, I was still the death doula who showed up for those left behind. I showed up for Maurice's life and the profound impact he had on those around him.

I changed lenses and snapped. I walked between mourners talking about their time with Maurice over the past twenty, thirty, and fifty years and discovered myself increasingly captivated by Maurice's being. Curiosity, an eternal driving force within me, prompted me to delve deeper. I snapped more and gave in to the loss of focus and assumed the role of a curious death doula, joining and sparking heartfelt conversations with the attendees, eager to piece together the mosaic of Maurice's life.

I'm a firm believer that there is no one we wouldn't extend a hug to if we knew their story. The smallest of their makeup heavily included. The stories I listened in on and instigated painted a portrait of Maurice as more than just a former marine; he was a beacon of compassion, resilience, and friendship to his friends and family. He was the kind of human I'd hug.

Maurice was more than two decades older, and Shelly's reminiscences of childhood summers spent in her favorite older cousin's company unveiled a tender bond forged through playful escapades in the hotel he owned, where they'd live and garden and share moments of innocence.

Shelly delivered the eulogy while I grabbed photos of husbands passing handkerchiefs, wives patting their husbands' knees signaling that it's okay to cry, and the American flag draped over the casket, reminding me of my best friend Nancy's father's casket in 2005, and my granddad's funeral in 2017. In Shelly's voice was poignancy and sincerity as she recounted anecdotes of their shared experiences, revealing one marked by acts of kindness and selflessness. Smack-dab in the middle of her tributes to his character, she acknowledged Maurice's role as a caretaker of stray cats and beautiful plants, embodying a spirit of compassion that transcended the boundaries of human interaction.

That moment of revelation reminded me of the power of storytelling to illuminate the hidden dimensions of a person's life. Storytelling at funerals is essential. It serves as one of the most powerful tools for honoring the dead, celebrating their life, and providing comfort to those left behind. It fosters a sense of connection and continuity, and it provides solace and strength to those mourning the loss while affirming the resilience and spirit of the community. When I think about Shelly's storytelling on this day, I am reminded to be grateful that I'm not only a death doula but a storyteller as well. In her tribute, Shelly extended gratitude to Larry, a man sitting in the last row in blue jeans, wheat-colored construction boots, and a black athletic shirt. Shelly thanked Larry for helping Maurice over the last few decades with caring for the hotel, the cats, and the garden, since she'd grown up and didn't come as often. With those words and the kind, familiar way others greeted Larry, I wondered why he sat in the back, barely noticeable, crying tears that didn't look like the tears of the friends in the front. George Eliot wouldn't be shocked that I could hear Larry's heartbeat. I stared for a while longer than I should have, and if I stared any longer, I'm certain I would have seen Larry's chest moving, too. Larry helped maintain the hotel and he cared for the cats, but Larry was not the help. It took me seconds to realize what no one else had. Larry was Maurice's lover, and no one sat with him. No one was there to tap his leg or hand him a handkerchief. This is when I cried with the mourners.

The eulogy ended with more smiles than it held in the beginning, and the funeral was done. I've always wondered why no one sticks around for the lowering of the body. This time was no exception. The grave diggers made their way toward the casket; and military friends, their wives, and Shelly all dispersed to partake in the rituals of remembrance at Maurice's favorite restaurant just across town. Larry stood as the grave diggers worked the crank, and I lingered under the bald cypress like the fragrance one wife wore that clung softly to the air long after the bloom has faded, waiting for the moment to approach Larry, a man visibly burdened by the weight of unspoken grief. He made his way toward his car, not noticing me being a creep just a few feet away, and I called for him. His brown skin was wrinkled and his eyes were red but wide with surprise. I stood just a couple of inches taller, but Larry looked like he may have been my height forty years ago. We stared at each other briefly, and before he could ask why I called him, I asked his permission to hug him. His face softened and maybe three wrinkles disappeared into the brown sea of his face. I offered him a simple gesture of solace—a hug that transcended the boundaries of conventionality, a silent acknowledgment of his pain and longing. Sometime over the last few years, I read about the unofficial Disney rule that a character will not release the hug until the visitor does, especially if it's a child. I didn't know about that rule when I hugged Larry, but I hugged him agreeing internally to not let go until he did.

In that hug I bore witness to the raw emotions that lay concealed beneath the veneer of composure. Larry's tears, a testament to the depth of his love for Maurice, flowed freely in the sanctuary of our shared understanding. Larry loosened his grip and so did I, then we talked. As Larry recounted fragments of their love story, I felt a profound sense of sorrow for Maurice, a man whose true and full essence remained partly shrouded in the silence of unspoken truths. Then I felt for Larry; once this day was over and I was gone, he would probably crawl back into himself and grieve in a way no one should—alone.

After the cemetery and the repast and the goodbyes to Maurice's friends and Shelly and a lover none of them would ever know was a lover, a profound truth emerged: the necessity of a death doula, even in the unlikeliest of roles. While my initial purpose was to simply capture moments through the lens of my camera, the depth of grief and the layers of untold stories surrounding Maurice's life demanded more. As I navigated the space between documenting and supporting, I realized that every person present, including myself, served as a conduit for the process of mourning. This experience underscored the vital role of storytelling in funerals, where narratives not only honor the deceased but also provide solace and strength to the bereaved. Shelly's heartfelt eulogy illuminated Maurice's multifaceted character, yet amid the shared memories and tributes there existed a realm of unspoken grief, as evidenced by Larry, whose presence went unnoticed by many. In a quiet moment beneath the bald cypress, I offered him a hug and a safe space to tell his own stories, to lighten his load, and to feel cared for, reaffirming the necessity of empathy and compassion in the face of death's silence. As Larry's tears mingled with mine, I recognized the profound significance of being present with a keen vision and feeling as a conduit for healing and understanding in the sacred space of grief.

If you ever find yourself in a moment where someone is quietly mourning, unsure of how to express their grief for fear of judgment, I want you to know how powerful your presence can be. Be that calm, steady presence in their life. You don't need to force a conversation; just let them know you're there for them. The simple gift of listening—without judgment or pressure—can be the most comforting thing you can offer.

Sometimes it's enough for them to know that someone cares and is willing to sit in that silence alongside them. And if they choose to open up, hold their words with the same tenderness you'd want yours to be held. Remember, they've been carrying a heavy load in silence, and it's not your role to fix or expose anything. Just let them feel seen, heard, and loved.

You have the power to make this part of their healing journey not so heavy.

DELPHINE

I'M UNCLEAR ABOUT THE CIRCUMSTANCES, THE PEOPLE, the insanity, or the foolishness that brought Michele and I together as friends when we were students at Bethune-Cookman University, but whatever it was, I'm grateful. She is of those friends I call when I need one of those laughs that hurts so good. The kind that blurs everything because of the tears they bring. We all need those friends. I was the funny, skinny frat boy with a big head and bigger mouth who did poetry on the yard and homework behind my friends' backs, hoping they never discovered how studious I truly was. Michele was the popular sorority girl in the band with one of those faces that made everyone smile when they saw her. She carries that beautiful spirit around like breath mints. I'd always joke, "You were raised right," a saying I heard from old folks when I was growing up, meaning "someone instilled in you a whole bunch of integrity and other things we should require of all of humanity."

Friendships like ours, especially when its foundation was built at a historically Black college, turned into a relationship more familial. If not siblings, then we are most definitely play cousins, a concept in the Black community that occupies a deeply cherished space, serving as a testament to the enduring bonds of community and kinship. Our relationships with play cousins are rooted in love, trust, and shared experiences.

Proving correct my theory of her upbringing, Michele finally introduced me to her mother, Delphine, via Facebook, or perhaps I caught a name in a post and added her as a friend myself. Either way, it didn't take long to see that behind Michele's unwavering character was a mother equally remarkable. Delphine's presence, albeit initially virtual, radiated a warmth and humor I've somehow been lucky enough to receive from the mothers of all my friends. But it wasn't until I met Delphine in person that I truly understood the depth of her being.

I'm grateful that I look for people outside of who they are in relation to others. Delphine wasn't just my friend's mother; she was an adventurer, fearlessly exploring on her bike every nook and cranny inside and outside of the Interstate 285 perimeter that encircles Atlanta. For me, Delphine was goals, even though my eating habits and physical activity routine would lead someone to believe otherwise. Who she was online was incredible, but it was when I drove to Lithonia to sit with her, taking down slice after slice of her favorite pizza, chasing it with some wine I'd gotten as a gift from a recent visitor, that I realized the extent of her keenness and magic. I often joked with Michele that if ever given the opportunity,

I'd jump to be her stepfather, and connecting with Delphine in person made my jokes louder and more frequent. Her visage reminded me of Danielle Joy Mckinney's paintings of Black women at rest. In her complexion of warm earth tones, a mole perched beneath her left eye, or perhaps it was a mark that would have told stories of escapades akin to those etched by intrepid adventurers and seekers of joy in the realm of childhood reveries. A gentle gap between her teeth she exposed when she talked or smiled or chewed with her mouth open reminded me of the pause between verses in some of my favorite songs, where the melody lingers, teasing of what's to come. She had a dimple reminiscent of innocent infatuations of her daughter during our college days. Delphine had a playfulness that stirred echoes of every childhood crush I held dear. On top of it all, and effortlessly, she blended care with humor that left me in awe, hoping that wouldn't be our last visit.

Life has a way of reminding us of its tenderness. In October 2023, Michele and I missed each other at our college homecoming, which rarely happens as we tend to make sure that among all the people we need to hug and laugh with, we are on each other's calendars. She was in and out, needing to get back to Georgia for something more pressing than a pep rally, a tailgate, sorority chants, and galas. Homecoming at a historically Black college and university (HBCU) is more than just a football game and tailgating. There was a quote circulating on social media with an unknown source that said,

"Homecoming at an HBCU is a family reunion, a block party, a cookout, a revival, a Black power rally, a spiritual and physical baptism in pure Blackness." Because it truly is all of these things, I'm normally loud when the people I love decide to sit it out or only attend in parts. But Michele's absence was different, and it was my keen feeling that told me to be silent and wait.

Just after returning home to my cabin in Georgia from Daytona Beach, Michele called with news of Delphine's leukemia diagnosis, and the ground beneath us trembled. It doesn't matter how long I've been doing this work or how many people I've helped usher to the other side, the initial moment after receiving news like that will always shock me and the words that come from my mouth are usually proof of that. "People like Delphine don't get sick," I said, quickly realizing it was untrue. In fact, I have many clients who, by most people's definition of fairness, shouldn't get sick and die of anything but old age. Being a death worker will make one reevaluate their notions of "fair."

Michele walked me through the days leading up to diagnosis as I sat on the other end of the phone silently changing out of my friend clothing and into my death doula threads. There was a brief silence when Michele stopped talking that I'm sure we both knew was necessary. She'd had days with this news, and I'd only had the last four minutes. I broke that silence with, "How does your mom feel?"

"She's ready," Michele responded, her tone telling me

she'd sat with that for some time before being able to speak it out loud. Another silence before I asked Michele how she felt about her mom's decision to not dance with cancer but with the inevitable. "I don't want to lose my mom," Michele said with a pause following, and before I could say anything, she added, "but I will respect her decision." As a death doula in that moment, I knew where to meet Delphine and Michele with any resources, assistance, and words I could gather.

Delphine's readiness to embrace the end of her life wasn't unique, but it demanded a level of acceptance and support that transcended personal desires; a level of support that, unlike Delphine's acceptance, is unique. Too often I've seen family members and friends, even those who hold the complete trust of the person actively dying, go against the wishes of that person in order to serve their personal desires. Michele's willingness to honor her mother's choice, even in its extreme difficulty, underscored the importance of respecting an individual's autonomy, especially in what would be their final moments. By listening to Delphine, Michele navigated a path fraught with uncertainty, transforming potential discord into cherished moments of connection. Not everyone who deeply loves the person reaching the end of their life takes this stance. As a death doula, I work hard to get everyone to understand the importance of listening while also understanding why they don't want to. Sadly, however, what I've seen and will undoubtedly continue to see while doing death work is that the people who spend their time attempting to get the actively dying person to change their mind and fight regret wasting so much of that invaluable time in contention.

In the days, then weeks, then months that followed, Michele, unsure of how much time she'd have with her mother, became Delphine's caregiver with grace. And through informal weekly check-ins, I set out to provide solace and assistance, recognizing the toll caregiving, especially in the end, exacts on the mind, body, and spirit. So often, when deep in the trenches of caregiving, folks aren't so sure what it is they need outside of rest and respite. This was Michele—unsure, exhausted, but hanging out with the help of an incredible husband and their two daughters. Thank goodness for support systems. As a friend, a person who loved Delphine, and a caregiver who understands the importance of self-care, I called Shannon, my friend from college and Michele's Delta Sigma Theta Sorority sister, and together we rallied support from our Bethune-Cookman University Wildcat community, assembling care packages tailored to Delphine's and Michele's needs.

Delphine's package, adorned with comforting essentials for the journey she was on—a knitted blanket that felt like a hug when covering the body, electrolyte drops for immunity support and hydration, lavender-scented Epsom salt for soaking, and a journal—symbolized our collective embrace, offering warmth and solace in her final days. For Michele, we put together an album of gift certificates to use when she found herself needing food and certainly didn't have the energy to cook or even think about where to go. If she needed a tea or a coffee or a croissant to keep going or to attempt to calm her nerves, there were certificates for that. And when she needed something for herself for no reason other than to be distracted, she was covered there, too. This was a gesture of solidarity and love, a reminder that neither of them was alone in this journey. We simply did what friends and family do. We take care of each other. As a death doula, I witness this outpouring of support and my belief in the power of community, especially in moments of profound vulnerability, is affirmed.

What's always been interesting to me, and what Delphine's transitioning brought back into my thoughts, is how quickly we accept death when we realize it's truly inevitable. I remember standing on the edge of a bridge railing in Baños, Ecuador, with a harness around my midsection, being told to jump by the man whose hands were holding my ankles. I knew that just a week before, a man died in this very spot doing this very thing, but the thrill seeker in me couldn't resist. I leaped, and as soon as my feet left the ledge, I heard the man yell, "Oh shit, I forgot to strap you in!" Without hesitation, I opened my arms as if I were Greg Louganis in Madrid in 1986, and watched as a memory from a beautiful beach in Curaçao played back to me. I was ready. When the rope snatched me back, I was equally fine knowing I had more time to experience more beautiful things. But in that suspended moment, I found solace in acceptance, much like Delphine did in her final days. Life, like bungee jumping in Baños, demands a leap of faith, a willingness to embrace the unknown. Knowing Delphine at her end leads me to believe death requires the same.

Delphine died on New Year's Eve, just before toasting a new year with the red wine Michele brought to her room, marking the culmination of a journey fraught with more beauty than pain. In her daughter's embrace she found solace, surrounded by love till her last breath.

In honoring Delphine's wishes, Michele transcended grief in a way that didn't cure her, but allowed her to move beyond it for a little while so she could embrace life's final act with courage. A sacred shift happened, and if we're fortunate enough when the end is near for our parents, we will experience it like Michele did. It will be like watching our own story replaying in reverse. Once, it was our parents or grandparents or aunts or uncles who held us close, guiding us through life's first steps. Now, in those final moments of theirs, it's our turn to hold their hands, to be there for them as they once were for us, navigating the final chapters together.

MELVA

I MET DENNIS KARL BROWN JR. IN THE FALL OF 2002 when we returned to Bethune-Cookman University to not only begin our junior year but also to pledge Kappa Alpha Psi Fraternity, a goal of mine since I was twelve years old and my first mentors, members of this same fraternity, came into my life and never left. To understand how strong the bond is between me and Dennis, it's important that I let you in on why the pledging process is necessary.

Beyond rituals and traditions, the pledging process serves, at least then, as a kind of hell that forges unbreakable bonds of fellowship among members. It is through shared experiences and challenges that create a sense of solidarity, and the triumphs endured throughout the process, that the individuals transcend mere acquaintanceship and become part of a cohesive unit bound by loyalty, mutual respect, and love. All of this fosters a lifelong brotherhood—or sisterhood, where sororities are concerned—rooted in shared values and a collective commitment to support and hold each other up through life's trials and tribulations.

Dennis and I walked through hell together and came out victorious.

We crossed over into the fraternity on December 11, 2002, at 3:04 a.m., and from that moment on, especially during our student days, Dennis and I navigated the highs and lows of life together. I was there when his hairline began receding and he needed to cut his signature shoulder-length, reddish boy-band braids. When I was going to become a father at twenty-two years old, Dennis was the person I shared the news with. I trusted him—and still do—with any secret I have, and I know it's mutual. We've sat in dark rooms while he reminisced on a failing, then eventual failed relationship with the girl he left in St. Louis. We're decades beyond that and can laugh about it now, remembering the sadness expressed while pouring cheap liquor from bottles our college budgets could barely afford. I don't remember when we stopped talking about his ex or picking out the most disrespectful songs to dedicate to her in her absence, but I do remember when Dennis started talking about someone new—Melva Crutchfield.

Melva arrived in our lives before Dennis's hair disappeared, and she spent hours sitting on the top of a picnic table, greasing his scalp and braiding his hair, while he sat on the seat between her legs. As the unofficial historian who knew these moments would one day be the ones I missed most, I snapped a photo of one of these braiding sessions, and it will always be one of my favorite of those two. I never trusted his style of flirting would attract anyone, but I was wrong and gladly accepted defeat.

After graduation, Dennis returned to St. Louis, and Melva made her way home to southern Florida. After a few years of road tripping and putting flights on credit cards, traveling to see the other, Melva packed up her things and moved to St. Louis.

It was homecoming season, and I landed in Daytona on a Wednesday in 2009, ready for the foolishness and skullduggery that always found me when I returned to that city with those frat brothers and friends I loved dearly. Dennis and Melva were arriving the following day, flying into Orlando's airport. After much begging from Dennis and some easy convincing from Melva, volunteered to drive the forty-five minutes to pick them up.

On Wednesday night, Dennis called to make sure the pickup was still planned. After I passed the phone around to every brother in the room to let him know just what kind of craziness he was flying into the following day, he told me that he'd been trying to get in touch with Melva all day. He even called the police, but they couldn't go into her apartment without the landlord's permission if there was no proof of necessity. To ease his mind, I told him I was sure she was fine, probably just phone issues, and hung up just after demanding he didn't miss his flight.

None of the five alarms I set between partying all night

and passing out on one brother's couch woke me up. It was the old-school house-phone-like ringer blaring in my ear. Dennis was calling. I answered and offered no hello or warm greeting. In exchange for waking me up, I jumped straight to "Please tell me you didn't miss your flight." This was the weekend we all could pretend we were undergrads again, and I, a twenty-seven-year-old feeling stagnant in a life I didn't intentionally build and simultaneously parenting an almost five-year-old at the time, needed every second to count.

I looked at the clock, waiting for Dennis to respond, realizing it was too early in the morning for them to have missed their flight. Before I could press the issue, still in my half sleep, Dennis quietly said, "She died." I could feel the weight of the words crushing him, knowing it was the first time he'd said them out loud. I was now fully awake, but nothing made sense. "Who died?" I asked, hoping he'd tell me it was the Chevy Impala he loved so much and talked about, as we all do, as though it were female. The prolonged silence told me it wasn't the car.

"Melva. Melva died." And there it was, laid out in front of us. There was silence between us as I pulled myself up to sit, but I listened to the noise behind Dennis, attempting to make sense of what he said and what those noisemakers were doing.

I asked him, "What do you need?"

In 2009 I wasn't calling myself a death doula, and I hadn't told anyone I worked in the death space. I was only moving along with what felt right within, with what felt like purpose. These days, now that I'm doing the work with intention, "What do you need?" is rarely my first question to folks who just lost someone very close, because most times they have no idea and I don't want them to feel like they have to figure it out at that moment. But I asked Dennis because I knew he'd know. We'd been in a hell before—though not this dark, it was a hell nonetheless.

"Can you call her sorority sisters? I don't think I can." We took a deep breath and I told him I'd call him back, and I stared at the phone for a second.

Through the years and over the course of Dennis and Melva's relationship, Dennis and I formed bonds with the women Melva pledged alongside, and now I needed to tell them their sister died. I called Andrea first, and how I delivered the news then, before officially doing death work, is how I deliver the news to the family and friends of the deceased as a death doula now—with deep compassion and empathy. Whether it's in person, on the phone, or in a message, I create a space for the receiver to grapple with the shock and sorrow of the news, and in that space I offer a listening ear and a comforting presence. Andrea was at work, welcoming students into her classroom when she answered. It felt wrong to tell her then, but after telling her to find a seat, it all poured out. She was silent, and I heard a student ask why she was crying. I told her what I knew and remained in the space I created until she could breathe.

I never called Dennis back. The hours after that initial call are a blur, but I remember three things. The first is how the brothers who'd already made it to Daytona to reenact the days that made them legends changed their plans to find Melva's sisters on the campus and sit with them, wrap their arms around them, feed them, and listen. The second is the conversation with Caroline at a St. Louis White Castle about the audacity of not putting mustard on burgers, even if they were sliders. The third is Dennis's face when he opened the door and found me there with a bottle of Appleton Estate rum. It wasn't until that moment that I realized I never called him back. I never told him I was coming. Honestly, it didn't feel like I'd traveled far, as if I'd wanted to be there with Dennis and magically appeared. "I don't know what we're going to do for the next few days, but I think whatever it is, we'll need this," I said, holding up the bottle and walking past him into his apartment, setting up the space I'd be holding for my brother as long as he needed.

Holding space for Dennis was no different from holding space for other grievers. Each time, even now, it requires a deep understanding of the complexities of the human experience. For me, in Dennis's apartment and in my work now, holding space is not about trying to fix or solve the grieving person's problems because grief is a natural, deeply personal response to loss. In it, however deep, the griever is dancing with thoughts, emotions, and experiences that not only are uniquely theirs but that also could crush them. Grief cannot be fixed. Holding space is not offering unsolicited advice or minimizing their pain or imposing one's own beliefs or experiences onto the griever. It's not about rushing the grieving process or showing up with a timeline for the griever to follow. It's opening the space for difficult emotions and uncomfortable conversations. It is not about finding quotes or foods or events to help the griever "get over it." Holding space isn't about making the situation about oneself or seeking validation for one's own feelings. It's not about pressuring the grieving person to "move on." Instead, it's about creating a supportive and nonjudgmental space where everyone who enters feels safe to explore and express themselves, knowing they will be heard, valued, and supported without reservation.

"Why'd you come?" Dennis asked, letting me know it wasn't that he didn't want me there but it was a surprise.

"What else was I supposed to do? Let you go through this hell by yourself?" I replied. And suddenly I was reminded of the story of two of our fraternity's founders. In 1912, Elder Watson Diggs married the love his life, his childhood sweetheart, Clara Bell Smith, but less than a year later, she died. Diggs asked John Milton Lee to join him at the funeral, and he did. As Diggs poured his heart out, Lee listened and offered a shoulder to his brother in need. In *The Story of Kappa Alpha Psi*, Brother William L. Crump wrote, "In this highly emotional atmosphere, Lee was impressed by the closeness between Diggs and himself engendered by the Fraternity. That Diggs should turn to him in this his greatest crisis gave new insight into the meaning of brotherhood."*

Dennis and I spent nearly a week together before I had to return home to DC to pack another bag, then head back to Florida for the funeral. When Dennis wanted to talk about Melva, we talked about her. When he wanted a random distraction, I found a man in a basement-unit apartment to tattoo me in exchange for a broken laptop, and I had Dennis drive us. When Melva's parents and sister came to clear out her apartment, we joined them, and I took the lead on conversations about the most random things—trying to keep the space from closing in on us. It closed in on us anyway, and together we all grieved.

Clearing out someone's space after they've died is one of the hardest things we can do. It's not just about the physical labor of packing boxes, removing shelves from the wall, and hauling furniture. It's walking into rooms that still feel like they're waiting for the person to return. Every item we touch holds their presence—the clothes they wore, the books they never got to finish, their favorite spoon in the drawer. And that weight? It's the kind of heavy that plants itself in your bones. But we did it together, leaning on each other as the grief crept in like a tide. Each box was more than just a collection of

---

* "Grim Interlude for Diggs," in *The Story of Kappa Alpha Psi: 1911–1983* (Philadelphia: Kappa Alpha Psi Fraternity, 1983), 14.

belongings—it was a piece of a life that was gone. We had to take our time, reminding each other to breathe, to take breaks when it got to be too much.

If you're clearing out the home of someone who has died, remember that it is not a task you can rush. It's emotional, and it's exhausting. Start small. Tackle one room at a time. One corner at a time, if you need to. Have boxes or bags labeled: Keep, Donate, Trash. Before you even touch anything, take a moment to stand in the space and breathe. Don't feel like you have to make decisions about every item right away. If something is too hard to handle in the moment, set it aside for later. Bring people you trust to help, and if you don't have that, give yourself permission to take your time. Play music if it helps, and take breaks often. You're not just cleaning a house; you're also honoring someone's life and navigating your grief.

One of the hardest moments that night was watching Melva's father as he quietly excused himself, needing space from the suffocating closeness of the apartment. He said he needed air, and no one questioned it because we all understood. He needed to be alone with his grief, to walk around the block, to cry where no one could see him. It was something none of us could carry for him, as much as we wanted to. When he returned, we didn't push him to talk—we continued cleaning and packing, making space for his pain without making it the focus.

Grief is never easy. It twists and turns, pulls you under, then lets you up for air, just to remind you it's not done with you yet. Dennis and I walked that winding road together, just as we had so many years before, but this time it wasn't about crossing over into a brotherhood—it was about crossing over through loss and learning how to live with it.

In the end, the bonds we forge in life are what carry us through these moments. The people who show up for us in our darkest hours are the ones who make the weight of grief bearable. They help us hold the memories, pack up the rooms, and sit with the silence when words aren't enough.

IRENE ELIZABETH JONES

MY GRANDMOTHER IRENE ELIZABETH JONES, WHO brought light to the path that nine-year-old me would walk, reached the end of her life and I was unable to get her the death she told me she wanted—many times, over cups of coffee that tasted more like tiramisu than Folgers and card games we'd play for whatever change we had in our pockets. But I was able to give her the permission she needed to leave this world behind.

Tiptoeing around death was something neither of us were accustomed to, even when the people around us gritted their teeth in discomfort—always loud enough to be heard. Or when they left the room with their hands over their ears, hoping that avoiding the conversation meant avoiding their end, and of course it never meant that. Many of them are dead now.

Some of my earliest memories of my grandma are her attending a funeral or sitting at the deathbed of a loved one. And every so often, sadly, I'd have a name to throw into the conversation. I remember my fifth-grade health teacher who died by suicide after a bad breakup. While the tragedy found itself into a few jokes from some of the older men in the family, who only knew how to talk about death when it was entertaining, my grandmother found a way to help me process my thoughts and emotions around it. And when my young understanding allowed me, I did the same for her. In a family of folks who were as scared of conversations about death as they were about death itself, the two of us found comfort in each other. Looking back, I suspect she saw me as the one who'd advocate for her, should any of her three children (my dad being the middle child) decide to ignore her wishes when the time came.

Above my grandma's couch (the couch I blame for always choosing couches over beds when it's time to sleep now), hanging from a nail hammered into the painted cinderblock, was a black-and-white photo of my great-grandmother in a fur coat. I remember looking up at it when my grandma told me she'd be ready to die the moment she could no longer enjoy life. I remember wondering if the woman in the photo thought the same thing. When she was no longer able to wear that fur coat and go dancing, did she just up and die?

I knew so little about the end of her life, and young me had questions I didn't know how to ask—not because there would be an awkwardness about it; I didn't have the language at the time. But I could ask my grandma about her own death and what she wanted in a way that made sense for me, so I did.

"When will you know you aren't enjoying it anymore?" I asked her.

She said it'd be when she could no longer dance in the kitchen with Bernard, her longtime beau who was very much a grandfather to me, while he was drunk and after she'd been sipping a little herself. Weekends in that kitchen were my favorite because he'd sing her favorite Billy Paul song, "Me and Mrs. Jones," off-key, loudly, and lovingly. Bernard was the love of her life and one of her favorite people on good days. On the bad days he caused, he knew to stay out of the house until the music played. She went on to tell me that when hamburgers with gravy and country fried potatoes lost their flavor, and when she could no longer play cards with the folks she'd sit around her living room table with almost daily, slapping down cards and coins while accusing each other of cheating, she'd be ready to go. "Before the old folks' home gets me," she said. She'd seen many friends die in hospices disguised as senior living facilities, and she didn't want it.

Like most of us, my grandmother wanted to die at home, peacefully in her sleep, and when the grievers were ready, her body would be cleaned, then dressed and put in her living room for family and friends to see how good she looked when they came to pay their respects. I made up my mind right there that I'd grow up, get a home big enough for me and my grandma and whoever I decided to love, and I'd make sure her death happened the way she wanted.

It didn't happen that way. My grandmother had been a diabetic for as long as I'd known and loved her, and her health declined to a point where family thought it was best to put her in the "old folks' home" she hated so much. I was somewhere in LA, starving, sleeping on couches, wondering how I'd eat while trying to make a name for myself. I couldn't afford the house she could die in, and I couldn't afford to keep her out of the place those around her thought it was best she be in. But I could afford a ticket home to be with her immediately after my mom called to tell me that my grandma stopped eating. I thought about the hamburgers and gravy with country fried potatoes, and I knew what was coming sooner than later. My grandmother's body was doing the dance that, if we're all lucky enough, we'll experience: it was shutting down, and eating was no longer necessary for it. Her body was saving the energy it would normally use to eat and digest for what it now found necessary. My grandmother and her body were preparing to die.

The body has an incredible wisdom, a kind of self-preservation instinct that allows it to begin the process of letting go, releasing all that is no longer needed. It's a poignant dance, one that mirrors the beauty of life itself. Muscles relax, metabolism slows, and the spirit begins its quiet ascent into the unknown. There's a peace that envelops everything, a soft surrender to the inevitable. I could see in her face the traces of a life well lived, lines etched from not just age but also laughter, smiling at those she loved each time they entered a room, and the weight of memories.

I can't remember how long I was home before she died. Sometimes when I think about her in that bed, unresponsive, not eating or talking or laughing or being who she always was to me, it feels like months. But other times when I think about who and what she was—the greatest human I'd ever known—it feels like only seconds that I got to spend with her. However long, I was there every day, holding her hands, grateful someone still came by to paint her nails. She often wore a deep shade of red on them, and I can always spot it when I'm out, no matter who's wearing it. I'd name it after her if I could. In that room I welcomed her friends who came to see her and offer their hopes of miracles and blessings I knew wouldn't come and I knew she wouldn't accept. I played "Me and Mrs. Jones" and hoped she was at least dancing in her head, or better yet, with Bernard, who'd died a few years earlier. She was love, and every day I sat there eased the guilt I felt for being the one person who'd give her exactly what she wanted at this time in her life if only I had the ability to do so.

She died years too soon. The person I became, the person I am now, would build the home she wanted to die in and bring her to it. I'd call my cousins she helped raise, and together we'd cry while we washed her body, performing the final act of care for the woman who loved us with her whole being. We'd put her in a dress—one she'd wear to one of those cabarets she loved. We'd give her gold dangling earrings to match. Her nails would be painted that deep shade of red, and we'd surround her with the flowers she loved and photos that prove she lived a life worth living. Those she loved most would come by to say what's on their hearts and everything they wish they'd said when she was alive.

The day my grandmother died, I was not yet calling myself a death doula, but I was. When I sat next to her bed each day, when I welcomed folks in to see her and helped them through their grief, when I relieved the people who were visiting when I arrived, I was doing it because the woman lying there taught me how. In the song "I Want You," the rapper Common says, "I love this way 'cause I got it as a kid." I loved my grandmother in that room because she showed me how. More importantly, I did all this because she was my grandmother. Even though I did not know then that I was a death doula, looking back now as one, I wouldn't have done anything differently given the resources I had then.

I remember my last visit with her. It was just the two of us and a clock that ticked a bit too loudly. I held her hand and told her I had no idea what I'd do with those I fell in love with. I always knew I was in love or at least I thought something incredible was forming when I wanted my grandmother to meet them. I asked her what I'd do with them now, and I laughed thinking she'd laugh at that. Then there was silence. I thought about all our conversations over the years and squeezed her hand and said, "I'm sorry I am not able to give you the death you wanted, but if you need permission to die, I can give you that."

I knew she was waiting, holding on to something. Perhaps she simply needed to know we'd be fine without her. One thing I know for certain is that grandmas, especially mine, are gifts. They are global treasures. I lied and told her we would be okay, knowing we wouldn't be, but we'd do our best.

"Everyone who wanted to see you and everyone who needed to see you has come. It's a beautiful day out." There was nothing else. "If you want to die today, you should. I love you. I'm going to play you a song and I'll leave you to it." Those were my last words to my grandmother. I played Coldplay's "Fix You" (the live from Arnhem, Netherlands, version), squeezed her hand, and left, knowing I needed to—or perhaps I wanted to be with my dad when the news inevitably came.

It took me fifteen minutes to get to my dad's place. I walked in, and before I could let out the sigh I'd been holding in since leaving the hospice, the house phone rang. I knew who it was and what they wanted. My stepmom answered. After "Hello" and a few seconds of nothing from her, she said what I knew she would: "Okay." She hung up, came into the living room, and told me my grandma was dead.

One night when I was sixteen years old, I sat in a McDonalds, softly crying over a box of Chicken McNuggets and a pack of sweet-and-sour sauce, thinking about the moment I'd get the news my grandmother was dead. At the time, I didn't know why I was crying. There was no threat of her dying then—thirteen years before she actually did. I suppose I was imagining a world without her, even though I didn't want to. Thirteen years later, when it actually happened, I didn't cry. I smiled, grateful that I could give my grandma that one thing she needed when everything else wasn't possible—permission.

LEON

THE DUST WAS AS CLOSE TO PERFECT AS DESERT DUST had been all week, and a dome of unbroken blue stretched above over the arid expanse of the Black Rock Desert. But as the final days of Burning Man unfolded, an unexpected twist of fate came in the form of rain—an unusual and unwelcome guest. This was only my second year celebrating creativity and self-expression with these good people, but looking at their faces as we watched the dusty terrain turn into a muddy quagmire, I knew the steady rainfall wasn't good. The once-vibrant playa had become a sea of rain-soaked tents and tarps.

After two hours into the rainfall, I found myself at the Camp Morning Wood bar, a haven in the tempest where me and other Burners gathered to find solace and plastic bags to tie around shoes, and to share stories. I huddled beneath the tarp, ankle-deep in mud, nursing a lukewarm cup of applesauce, plucking peanuts into my mouth as I became more accepting of being potentially stranded in this surreal desert city for a week longer than planned. The rain had transformed

Black Rock City into an island, cut off from the outside world by a sea of mud and uncertainty.

As I exchanged wary glances with my fellow Burners and poured shots of Fireball for the passersby, my attention was pulled by a man standing nearby, loudly asking why I was wearing a tutu. Burners who were also strangers to him immediately called him Baby Vin Diesel because his build, face, voice, and command of attention were very much like the actor. I couldn't help but respond, telling him, "Because I look amazing in it." Baby Vin Diesel wore a zipped-up sweatshirt that dripped water everywhere he walked, not that it mattered. His eyes moved slowly when he spoke and held a quiet fire and a hint of mischief.

While I waited at the bar for a few of my camp mates so we could walk around the playa and play in the mud and find the Whitney Houston party we'd been hearing so much about, Baby Vin Diesel and I exchanged more slick talk and poured more of whatever we could find into our cups. He poured alcohol, I poured juice, and conversation topics changed with each sip. He'd yell obscenities to whoever was in earshot, and I did my best to convince them it was the liquor talking. He reminded me of my brother, Dennis, and we were somehow united by a shared sense of camaraderie born from our predicament—a desire to find any distraction from the looming uncertainty. The way he spoke of the unpredictable nature of everything led me to believe he was an outdoorsman. "Never trust nature," he said. "It'll turn on you in an instant." The honesty and ease in his tone sounded like he was talking about his friends.

A fellow Burner, drenched and slightly shivering, carried his bike toward us, trying his hardest not to slip in the playa mud. He planted the bike next to us and said he had a dry, warm shirt in one of his bag pockets and needed help. Without hesitation, Baby Vin Diesel—who'd just finished playfully cursing out another Burner who was in active panic mode, wondering if they'd make it home to their dog—sprang into action.

He grabbed the man's bike, easing his load, and made a few jokes to help the man change his attitude. It worked. The man smiled, and even I laughed. He then helped the man out of the wet body shirt and into the dry thermal. It would stay dry long enough to get the man where he was going, he said. That moment, their exchange, spoke to the spirit of community that burned at the heart of Burning Man. It was in that moment—his simple act of kindness—that I unknowingly captured the last photograph of this loud, funny, obscene man.

Me and my camp mates, one dressed as a pickle and another as a penguin, and me in a tutu, left for our journey. We came back three hours later to a somber camp talking about the death of a man who'd stopped by earlier. He'd died on the road, next to a camper parked at our camp. No one knew what happened exactly. Thirty minutes passed before we learned it was Baby Vin Diesel who died in the mud.

The transient nature of Burning Man, with its limited phone service and remote location, made me question how his family would get the news. Thought after thought about who he could be outside of all the lights and bikes and art and music and mud came while I walked from person to person, listening to them talk through their grief, anxiety, fears, and similar concerns as mine. I didn't think I'd show up that weekend as a death doula, but there I was, being just that.

As the days passed and our food lockers were almost empty, we found a way out of the desert, and my thoughts remained with Baby Vin Diesel's family. I was haunted by the photograph I had taken, a wild but silent reminder at just how fleeting life is. It was a weight I couldn't shake, and the more I looked at it for signs of anything—sadness, a call for help, a look of relief in his eyes, anything—the more I knew I had to reach out to the people who loved him. I strung together some key words I figured news outlets would use and within minutes, Baby Vin Diesel's face was on my screen. There, I found his name was Leon and further down, I found his mother's name—Sharon. It was a heart-wrenching post about losing her child and a piece of a man's life.

Unsure of how she'd respond to a stranger contacting her about her son just days after his death, I reached out to Sharon. In a message, I introduced myself as a man who'd met her son in the mud. I told her about our conversations and laughs, and his outbursts and jokes. I told her how he helped the man change into warmer clothes while also making him laugh. I thought she'd want to know her son was laughing before it all happened and that he made someone warm and happy. She responded within minutes. Our exchange was a cascade of Sharon's tears and memories. While I was only able to fill her in on my last moments with him, she was able to fill me in on the parts of his life I wasn't there for, and I gave her space to keep writing and talking. It was a connection forged in grief, a lifeline for a mother who had been searching for answers.

I'm not sure why I was nervous to tell Sharon about the photo. I wondered if I would want to see what my child looked like moments before his death. I wasn't sure. We were at the end of our conversation and I asked if she wanted to see the photo. She immediately responded yes. The moment she saw her son's smiling face in that wet sweatshirt with the sun hitting him just right, she smiled. "This makes you family now," she said to me, and we both cried.

Sharon and her family drove to Black Rock City to see the place where her son died and to deepen the connection with him. She also hoped to find the memorial, created by a Burner named Geobender, on the spot where he took his last breaths. She called me from the playa searching for the design made of mud because she thought it would be at his camp, but it wasn't. The manmade city created to hold us Burners in the desert is fashioned after a clock, with streets running from 2:00 to 10:00. The avenues are letters, running from the Esplanade to the K. I told her to head to where 7:45 & E briefly existed but to have little expectations of seeing it, because I was sure the drivers had completely leveled the work of art. She wrote me as soon as she found it and sent a photo showing it was almost completely intact. The only thing missing was the flower.

An hour after learning of Baby Vin Diesel's death, I sat on the crib mattress in my SUV with covered windows thinking about what I'd do if my son died. What would I want to know about those moments or days leading up to his death? What did he do in those last moments? Was he happy? Where did it happen, and was he scared? Did something sweet pass his nose, and did something beautiful catch his eye? Everything I remembered and shared with Sharon was because I knew I'd want it, too.

As a death doula, I understand the profound importance of creating space for those who grieve. Sometimes that space is physical, as it was for my camp mates immediately following his death. Sometimes that space is silence over the phone while the person grieving gathers their thoughts and themselves, like with Sharon. I was asked during a panel, "What must we do with all the space we are holding for others and all the space we are creating?" It's in those spaces that we must connect. As a death doula, I am always connecting.

The story of Baby Vin Diesel, as he will always be called by me and my camp mates, is not just about the chance encounter at Burning Man, the last photograph, or the digital breadcrumbs that led me to his mother. It is a testament to the power of connection in the face of loss, the enduring impact one person can have on the lives of others, and the healing potential of empathy and compassion.

Even in the small role I played in helping Sharon make her way toward healing and closure, I couldn't help but reflect on the lessons this journey had taught me. Our existence here is fragile and beautiful and very much like that city we build in Nevada each year—transient and unpredictable, but created to be cherished.

I want to share something with you that I'm certain won't surprise you: Your stories, even the small ones, could mean the world to someone who's grieving. When a person passes away, those who loved them hold on to every bit of who they were. It's why it's difficult to throw away even the smallest of things that belonged to them. Sometimes the briefest encounters you had with that person—moments you might think are insignificant—can bring comfort, peace, or even joy to those left behind.

Baby Vin Diesel and I spent the smallest amount of time together, but after he died, sharing those moments with his mother meant more to her than I could have imagined.

Don't hesitate to reach out and share the memories you have. It could be as simple as a laugh you shared, a kind gesture they made, or even a conversation about the rain. Those little pieces of their life might be exactly what someone needs to hear to smile. You might just become a source of healing in their journey.

GRIEF AIN'T JUST ONE WAY

MARCUS PULLED ME ASIDE AT A HOOKAH LOUNGE in LA and asked something to the effect of "Ain't you that guy that helps people die?" I laughed as I always do when I hear this and said what I think I always have to say when this is someone's approach: "Yeah, but not in the sense of killing them." Marcus laughed back, introduced himself, then said, "I know, but do you also help the family after the person died?"

"A familiar question," I thought, having been asked by at least one out of every four people who find out I'm a death doula. For the conversation I knew was about to happen, I figured we'd need to take up space at the booth he was sitting in with his girlfriend or at my noisy booth with friends who dragged me out for the night insisting this hookah spot wasn't as cliché as all the poorly lit others filled with folks blowing thick clouds for Instagram photos. My friends were wrong. We took the conversation to Marcus's booth, and I let him talk after telling him that I do help the families after the death, if they want my help.

In the hookah lounge, while his girlfriend blew thick

clouds into her phone lens, and while my friends barely knew I was gone, Marcus asked for my help. He began telling me about the giant who was his father. Keith was a Southern Black man raised on old-school principles, meaning he not only knew everyone in the vicinity by name but he also asked how their parents were doing when he stopped the folks to talk. He raised his fingers when passing other cars: one finger for "How you doin'?"; two fingers for "How y'all doin'?"; three fingers for "How your mama 'nem?" He knew the importance of cooking too much food for dinner. No one went hungry in the sticks of South Carolina where he was from as long as they knew where he lived and had a way to get there. He sat on the porch and yelled to the neighbors, letting them know how nice the tomatoes they were growing looked, and he stood up at every family reunion to let people know his world-class fried whiting was ready to eat and to thank everyone for coming to celebrate family.

Marcus's accounts of Keith as a father were filled with stories of endless patience, sage advice, and love expressed through food, kisses on the top of their heads no matter how old his kids got, and words. If he missed any part of his kids' lives, there was a reason they could understand, and he'd still fight to make sure they were okay. Keith was a pillar, and having experienced him as a father and later in life as a friend, Marcus wanted to know why he hadn't yet grieved.

As a death doula, I hear this question more often than you might expect: "Why haven't I grieved yet?" It's one of the most common concerns people have when they don't experience grief in the ways they were told to expect, such as intense crying or feeling like they're being crushed in a stampede of sadness. I'm also approached by folks who say things like, "I have a friend who lost their mom, and I don't think they've fully grieved yet," and they're eager to find ways to help. I tell them grief doesn't follow a set script, and just because someone's not openly mourning doesn't mean they aren't feeling the weight of loss in their own unique way.

When people ask why they haven't grieved, what they're really asking is, "Why doesn't this look like what I imagined?" I remind them that grief is unpredictable. It's not something that follows a linear path or fits into a single box of emotions. We often have ideas about how grief is supposed to look because of how we've seen others experience it, or our ideas might have come from movies and books. Trust me, grief is there—it just shows up in ways we don't always recognize right away.

I asked him the question I don't think we ask enough: "What does grieving look like?" What Marcus was feeling and questioning is something I see often in the weeks and months and sometimes years following a death. The bereaved, in most cases, don't know to call the things they're doing and the feelings they're feeling "grief." If they do, they feel their grief isn't enough to offer up in return for the love they felt, and they look for more, whether they want more or not. "What does grieving look like?" Marcus looked for the same sadness and anger he felt when his best friend died when they were twelve years old, and he wondered what happened to the tears he thought would come at Keith's funeral and then again randomly while showering. He didn't get anxious, lose sleep, and or build a moat around himself—all things he'd done when losing someone he loved deeply, just not his father. Marcus felt guilt, but not the guilt that normally comes with grief—the guilt about things left unsaid and undone. Marcus's guilt was about his absence of guilt. It couldn't possibly be that everything he wanted to say to his father had been said. To him, that'd never been done in the history of fathers and sons.

Marcus stopped talking, then he pulled as much smoke from the hookah pipe as his lungs could stand and blew it in his girlfriend's face, making her laugh, reminding me she was there. He looked over to me, saying nothing, but his raised eyebrows asked, "Know what I mean?" I knew exactly what he meant and told him so. And I found myself silently thankful for the opportunity to tell him more about what I learned about grief from grievers who asked me as a doula to sit with them, as Marcus was doing now.

From Alisha—who still hasn't cried about the death of her favorite aunt (as of the time I last spoke with her)—I learned that grief sometimes looks like garden work. Some mornings, before getting ready for work and before the rest of her world is awake, Alisha gets her hands dirty in soil, planting new flowers, pulling weeds, and tending to her thyme, cucumbers, collards, and strawberries. Before she died, her aunt called her every morning to pray for her; to make sure she was having breakfast, since it was, as her aunt called it, "the meal of success"; and to talk about the plants and flowers hanging around her house—the ones she was struggling to keep alive, the ones she named after her favorite TV characters, and the ones that secretly gossiped about the others. When Alisha got the news of her aunt's sudden passing, the first thought she had was "What's going to happen to Virgil Tibbs, the succulent?" She laughed out loud to herself. She started a garden the next day, knowing nothing at all about gardening, and she said each new addition was a conversation with the woman who taught her to love the earth.

When Bobby got the call that his best friend, Quan, died in a motorcycle accident, he did something he'd never done: He went running. He made it a point to tell me he was in dress shoes, having just left work, but it was just a run around the block. When he walked back in the house, winded and with sharp pains moving through his calves and ankles, he googled marathons instead of dealing with the tragedy, knowing there'd be plenty of time to deal with that later. After seeing the total distance of a marathon, Bobby looked up local 5Ks and left the house, left his phone on the counter, and bought a pair of running shoes. Every mile he covered was a mile closer to dealing with the pain he thought he was putting off. He told me he'd get a message about funeral plans or see a "Sorry for your loss" message on his social media and he'd lace up his shoes and run. Each step, he said, brought memories that made him laugh. After the wake, Bobby ran. After the funeral, Bobby ran farther. And on the day of the 5K, he crossed the finish line, exhausted, overwhelmed, and completely in tears, laughing at how stupid Quan would say he looked at that moment. From Bobby I learned that grief also looks like running; it looks like sweat and laughing simultaneously.

The coals resting on the aluminum at the top of the hookah were nothing more than ash, and Marcus sat there, listening and nodding as his hands stroked his beard. "Grieving is more than one thing," I told him. It's the sadness, the anger, the tears, the guilt, the anxiety, the complete numbness. Grief is waking up in the middle of the night, it's never going to sleep, it's the tightening of the throat as if a hand were wrapped around it attempting to make a fist. But it's also laughter and singing and buying annuals to plant in our yard, thinking "annuals" means they'll grow back next spring, too. It's writing a memoir about our life with that person who died and the lessons they taught us, like Franky did. It's playing our harmonicas loudly when words can't fully express what we need them to, like Monica did after her husband died. And there, on that couch with too many burn holes for my liking, Marcus realized the neighborhood potluck he puts together when he goes back to his hometown, the smiling at old-timers while driving through the neighborhood, and his efforts to keep things as his father left them—that was what grieving also looked like.

Please always remember that grief is often painted in heavy, dark strokes, but it doesn't have to be. It is more than just sadness; it's the way we continue to live, laugh, and remember. It's in the quiet moments when you make your grandmother's famous pie recipe, even if it's just for yourself. It's in the way you play your favorite song that reminds you of your best friend, singing out loud in the car. Grief is a part of love, and love isn't always just sadness.

The truth is, grief can be full of life.

When it comes to death and grief, never assume. That person who looks like "they haven't grieved yet" may be falling apart in private. Go to them, ask questions, listen, and support them.

BLACK MEN DON'T GRIEVE FOR THEMSELVES

BLACK MEN DON'T GRIEVE FOR THEMSELVES AND they don't mourn the coming end of their life. As of this writing, I've never been called to be a caregiver, to sit vigil, to advocate for, or to hold the hand of a Black man by a Black man himself. It's been the child, the wife, the sister, the niece, the cousin, and the hospice nurse of the Black man whose life is coming to a close who's called me to ask that I come. I've never been shocked by this. After all, I am a Black man who was raised around Black men and I've seen many of them at the end of their life, whether they knew it or not. Each time, the concern was on the faces of the friends and family members, but never the man. "What must that feel like," I wondered, "to have a foot so close to the grave and to pretend to feel nothing?"

Though these Black men have never asked for me directly and are often very reluctant at my first visits to open up, I am always grateful for the call. I am there to support them through the process of dying, and a large part of that means helping them to embrace their own mortality—because until they do, there is little acknowledgment of the reality they're facing. I've watched these men, some with only days left, deny and avoid their impending deaths like my South African taxi drivers ignore bright red lights at busy intersections in the middle of the night. This is the reality I've faced with clients like Jimmy, who denied his pancreatic cancer until two weeks before he died, leaving his bed in the middle of the night to cry alone and writhe in pain on the bathroom floor, away from his wife. And Mark, who literally had to be taken against his will to the hospital by his son because he believed as long as he didn't acknowledge the sickness or the death that was coming four days after being admitted, it wasn't real.

No matter the client, I start by cultivating trust and building a rapport through listening to them while they share stories of their life, their experiences, and their reasons for not trusting the medical system and those they feel are adjacent, sometimes including death doulas. I validate those experiences and give them the respect they deserve. In these spaces, it's extremely important for me to normalize emotional expression, and in doing this, I find myself helping them to challenge societal norms simply by asking questions like: "What emotions are easy for you to express and why do you think that is?" "Who told you that you couldn't cry?" "What pressure do you feel weighing down on you when you want to express certain emotions but choose to suppress them?"

In the spaces I share with Black men at the end of their

lives, I am just as much of a creative as I am a death doula. Presenting a creative outlet to my clients—some who are naturally creative already and may not know it—can provide a means of processing grief and connecting with the inner self they thought they lost on that last day of boyhood. There is a joy that comes to them and me when they find the pieces and put them back together. Getting them to the grieving allows them to release pent-up emotions such as fear, sadness, anger, and anxiety. When we get to this place and they give themselves permission to grieve, they free up space for light to enter. The greatest joy is in pain relieved.

Jimmy's wife, Lavonda, called the day after he told her he'd been diagnosed with pancreatic cancer. He'd known for months. After listening to the doctors tell him the only thing they'd be able to do for him at that point was make him comfortable, he decided he'd hold off on telling her and bear the concern for the two of them. But Lavonda knew something was wrong when Jimmy was getting up throughout the night and disappearing for nearly an hour each time, returning drenched in sweat and with a weak voice. After being married for twenty years, she knew that if Jimmy didn't mention it, she shouldn't bring it up. "I thought it was kidney stones," she told me. Working in the death space for as long as I have, I recognize pancreatic cancer as the cancer that leaves very little room for follow-up questions. Jimmy only told Lavonda because she came home earlier than planned and caught him packing a small duffel to escape the house they'd built together. He was on his way to warmer weather where he could die without questions. She made him tell her what was going on. She was sure there was another woman; she thought the stress of an affair could have caused the potential kidney stones. Jimmy stopped packing and sat next to Lavonda on the floor and poured out what he knew about his pancreatic cancer. She told me she thought about how some of her favorite celebrities had pancreatic cancer and they all died. She looked at Jimmy and said, "You wanted to die alone?" He didn't respond, and she knew that meant yes.

They called the doctor to find out what the doctor meant when they said all they could do was make Jimmy more comfortable. Then they picked up the medication, went to dinner, and came home to lie next to each other and laugh about Jimmy attempting to make a run for it. He didn't leave the bed that night. Instead, he let Lavonda rub his back and hold him. But he didn't cry, and he still talked very little about how he felt.

The next day, Lavonda called me—she was falling down the rabbit hole of google searches. The day after that, I was in their home, sitting across from her and Jimmy. At this point, Jimmy believed because he only had a little pain at night, death was as far away from him as it was for anyone else in the room, but I was sure to stress the importance of Jimmy grieving his illness, his circumstances, and the goals, life, and plans he would no longer fulfill. When I attempted to facilitate moments for self-reflection and opportunities for Jimmy to identify unresolved issues and regrets, he'd change the subject. When I asked about unfulfilled aspirations, Jimmy pretended he didn't hear me and talked about his mother's transition. He talked about being in the room when she died and how she looked toward the corner when she spoke to someone Jimmy couldn't see. "She told him she loved him, too, and she was ready," Jimmy explained. Jimmy's father was still alive, so the person she was speaking to couldn't have been him, Jimmy thought. His mother's first husband had died, leaving her a widow before meeting Jimmy's father. Jimmy believed that's who it was. Just as Jimmy was about to leave the room to get a bite to eat from the cafeteria downstairs, his mother died. Here was a way in.

"Who do you want to come back for you?" I asked. He heard me. His eyes darted toward mine and we held that eye contact for at least three long seconds, until he dropped his head and asked, "You believe in all that? Spirits and stuff?"

I told him I wouldn't be in this work if it weren't for the spirits guiding me to it.

"When was the last time you saw spirits?"

When I first arrived to death work with intention, I was very hesitant to mention my experiences with spirits and things some folks see as "otherworldly."

I told Jimmy about Sheena, a friend I met just three years before I met him. After sharing our death work experiences, Sheena called me a medium—a title I still haven't fully accepted. Sheena, however, *is* a medium, but there are limits to how spirits shows up for her. For me, the veil is especially lifted during mushroom ceremonies. Just a few weeks before Lavonda's call, I'd connected with Sheena hours before a mushroom ceremony on sacred land. It was a journey I had been looking forward to for months. Sheena was not joining me for the ceremony, but she wanted to send me off with good energy and ask a favor. She knew that during every one of my journeys, I'm approached by the spirits. Sometimes they need favors, and sometimes they just want to sit.

My fraternity brother Jonathan's dad, who I'd never met, came into my apartment in LA and asked me to hug his son. My cousin James came to my cabin and sat with me, asking me to tell his daughter Floshanda, one of my favorite cousins, that he apologizes for not being the father she deserved. Even my grandmother came for a visit and bathed me in a small tub in her kitchen sink while she shared her entire life story with me—her dreams, aspirations, and desires. I asked if the sacrifices she made were worth it, and she told me they absolutely were because she had me and my cousins. Then she asked me to share this with everyone except my cousin Jackie, because she'd never understand. She was right.

Sheena asked if, during the ceremony, I could ask her friend John to come visit me. He'd died a year before and his body wasn't found for several days. She wanted to know if he was okay. Initially I refused, telling Sheena I'd never asked spirits to visit me. They simply showed up without permission, but were welcomed nonetheless. Part of me didn't want to know if I could call them. Sheena asked again, and I relented.

That night, on that sacred land, the mushroom ceremony began with writing my intention in my journal, as I always do, directing my attention inward and giving purpose to my journey. My intentions have always provided emotional support during challenging moments on my journeys, helping me to interpret insights and feelings that surfaced. I wrote, "This journey is about being here for whoever may need me." Under that, remembering Sheena, I wrote, "John, if you need me, come." I grounded myself, meditated, then waited.

Shortly after time lost its meaning, the friend I shared the space with looked over to me and said, "There's a line of people here for you." I looked over toward the forest and there, in a line so long it curved, were countless Black men staring at me with deep emotion, as if waiting for me to call them up to speak. "I told you I was here for whatever you needed," I told them. "Let's go." I sat there, a vessel, while each man, one at a time, asked me to cry. One man squatted in front of me before climbing in and said, "I never got the chance to grieve myself. Thank you."

John showed up, but not until the crowd dispersed and I was nearly all cried out. "Tell Sheena I'm good," he said. "I'm only here to cry," and it was the most intense cry of the night. In prostration he stretched my arms out as though I was giving the ground a hug. Tears flowed like a rushing creek. While

I gave him permission to cry to completion, I remained present as well, sharing my body with the griever. When he was done, he left. Everything that followed was purely incredible and added to an already unforgettable trip, especially while reflecting on it all the following day during integration. Following every journey, I shift into the process of incorporating into my life everything I gathered on the trip—the insights, emotions, and revelations.

I found Sheena to share my experience with her, and before I could say anything, she asked, "Did John come?"

I nodded.

"Did he cry?" she asked.

With a look of surprise, I nodded again.

"Was it an ugly cry?"

I reached out and grabbed Sheena's hand, not sure how she knew any of it. "It was the ugliest cry I've ever had," I told her, showing her just how far my arms were stretched and how my forehead touched the earth.

Sheena laughed and blurted out, "That's John!"

I told her about all the Black men who stopped by to do nothing but cry because they felt like they weren't allowed to do it while alive. In my integration I realized that for me to continue in death work, especially when called to assist a Black man transitioning, I needed to develop my abilities to bring clients to grieving themselves.

Jimmy looked at me, nearly frozen, then said, "And here you are, about to make a Black man cry for himself." He smiled and said, "Damn, boy. That's why I only smoke weed," and we laughed.

Jimmy remembered every question he avoided and answered them. He hoped it was his mother who came back for him. He said if there is any justice in all the living and all the struggling and all the pain, she'd come for him with two fat ham biscuits in her hand. I wished that for him. And as he talked about the aspirations that never came to fruition, he cried.

Two weeks later, Lavonda called to tell me Jimmy died the night before, pain free and smiling after what she thinks was a good cry. She said their last little bit of time together will always exist among the most beautiful times of their marriage. Before hanging up, I asked who came back to get Jimmy. Lavonda said she had no idea, but whoever it was sure had him smiling.

I want to take a moment to speak directly to you, reader, and just Black men. Maybe you're here because you feel connected to the stories I've shared, or perhaps you're navigating your own path through grief, loss, or caregiving. Wherever you are on this journey, I want you to know that it's okay to grieve yourself, too. We often get so caught up in holding space for others that we forget we are worthy of the same attention, care, and grace.

Grief is not just something we feel for others—it's something we need to feel for ourselves. It's recognizing the parts of us that are changing, the dreams that didn't unfold, the versions of ourselves we lost along the way. For Black men especially, grief can feel like an unspoken language, something we're never taught to express, and yet it lives in our bodies, waiting to be acknowledged.

I've seen the power of what happens when men allow themselves to feel, to weep, to release the weight they've carried for far too long. It's not weakness; it's liberation. That release—whether it comes through tears, words, or simply sitting in the quiet—is one of the greatest acts of courage we can offer ourselves.

So, wherever you are, take a moment to pause. Give yourself permission to grieve your own losses, your unfulfilled hopes, and the person you once were. It doesn't matter how much time has passed, that grief is still yours to honor. As you do, you'll find space for the light to enter, space to breathe, and space to grow.

MISHA

IT WAS THE MIDDLE OF THE AFTERNOON IN THE PART of early autumn when the days are still long and bright and affable, but the bedroom where Misha and I sat across from each other was dark, like the rest of her mom's house, thanks to the closed blackout curtains in every window. There were no clocks, and the little pieces of light sweeping under the front doors created shadows on the bottoms of furniture and helped me keep track of time. Misha told me she was always short but never this skinny, making light of her frail body, at least the half sticking out from under the thick blanket. I joked back, telling her that if either of us were any bigger, we wouldn't fit in the room. She laughed, and her mother, Carolyn, came running at the sound of something so unfamiliar in the house. "It'd been a long time since Misha laughed," Carolyn said, asking what could have possibly been said to make it happen.

This wasn't a small house, and there were rooms much bigger than the one Misha chose to die in, but this was her childhood bedroom. She said it was the last place she felt completely herself. The pieces of the wall not covered by high school photos of Misha with her friends and old, torn-out magazine pages featuring Immature, Boyz II Men, Lil' Kim, and Jon B. were a light shade of yellow, and the wooden floorboards creaked under any pressure. The blackout curtains were heavy and velvetlike, and on closer examination, they were a deep purple. On the desk was a once-large pink bunny that can only be won playing amusement park games, but now it sat slumped over and half filled. The TV, which took up most of the desk space, and the hospital bed were the only new things in the room. And there was a globe—old, dusty, and out of place—sitting on a nightstand blocking the closet door.

The globe was a gift from her dad when Misha was ten years old. Since opening it, she wanted to be a flight attendant and go to all the places her dad would research and bring up casually, talking about them in vivid details as if he'd been there himself and his words were derived from memories. That was until Misha would catch on to his tall tales and they both laughed. She still dreamed. She'd have tea beneath a blossoming cherry tree in Kyoto with a boyfriend she met while traveling; and sit atop Table Mountain in Cape Town, having a picnic with all the friends from all the photos on her walls. They'd drink wine and laugh and talk about how short their dresses were going to be at the party that night. She was going to have a lei placed around her neck just as she stepped off the plane in Hawaii. She'd drink her dad's favorite beer in

Germany and send him a postcard with a photo on it of her holding the bottle. But she was dying now, seventeen years after opening that globe, and never made it out of the state.

Misha was diagnosed at twenty-seven years old with late-stage pancreatic cancer in mid-March, several weeks after leaving work early with a bellyache so intense, she had no choice but to go to the ER. She told me the pain that came with the diagnosis was the kind of pain that eventually numbs the body, starting with the tongue. She sat still, unable to lift the weight dropped on her—a weight neither her nor her mother sitting next to her could comprehend. How could this be happening to her, at her age, with three children? How does this happen to someone with a life full of responsibilities and dreams?

In the beginning, Misha handled the whirlwind of appointments and consultations with an unfathomable strength she attributes to the three little faces that waited for her at home, relying on a stability Misha was no longer sure of. She barely had time for herself these days, even before the diagnosis. She had no idea where she was going to find the time and strength for this battle. Life's greatest tests often come unannounced, but it's in those moments that we unearth power we didn't know we had.

Misha hadn't come close to the life she wanted, and she always thought she'd make up for it when the kids were older, when the car was paid off, after she found and bought the house she wanted, when she got the raise and promotion she deserved. None of these things happened, and because of that, Misha's will to survive increased exponentially and she dove headfirst into the unfamiliar world of pancreatic cancer. She ferociously devoured information, learning everything she possibly could about the disease, the pancreas, and even her medical team. She told me she called the medical schools some of them attended to see if she could get copies of their grades and reports. Google became her constant companion as she delved into every medical trial and research paper in search of hope.

The odds weren't in her favor. Pancreatic cancer is one of the most aggressive forms of cancer, often diagnosed at late stages when treatment options are extremely limited. At one of her earlier appointments, her father, fighting back tears, asked the doctor what survival looked like in this type of cancer. Misha wished he hadn't asked, but that didn't stop the doctor from answering. From that day forward, the survival statistics hung over Misha like a shadow, casting doubt on the possibility she would see her oldest kid reach his teen years. Yet she kept fighting.

In the five months that followed her diagnosis, Misha encountered both triumph and despair, each a testament to the unpredictability her readings told her to expect. And in the sweltering heat of August, Misha found herself confronting a truth she had long tried to evade: She was going to die. It was a realization that settled over her like the weighted blanket she now used as often as the pain meds. It was suffocating in its finality.

In the quiet moments of solitude, she allowed herself to acknowledge the gravity of her prognosis, to feel the weight of all she would leave behind. Yet amid the anguish and sorrow, there was a strange sense of peace—a resignation to the inevitable that brought with it a peculiar kind of liberation. In accepting the reality of her mortality, Misha found the freedom to savor each moment with a depth of gratitude she had never known before. It was a bittersweet revelation, tinged with sorrow and infused with a new, quiet strength that carried her through the remaining days with a sense of purpose and resolve.

A large part of that sorrow came from Misha making the difficult decision to have her children live with their father, while she moved back into the room where we met. Coming back to her childhood home, though necessary, was odd for Misha since it was the last place she existed without a care in the world. Here she was, back, with what felt like every care that ever existed.

In the months leading up to her death, the aggressive nature of the disease took its toll on Misha's body, leaving her drained and fatigued most of the day. Endless rounds of chemotherapy and radiation treatments became a routine part of her life, each session bringing with it a mix of hope for more days and apprehension. The side effects were relentless—nausea, hair loss, and debilitating weakness, and for a while, Misha soldiered on, determined to squeeze every moment out of the time she had left. But even soldiers get tired. It didn't take long for the guest list to shrink—not because people didn't want to see Misha but because Misha didn't want them to see her.

Carolyn found me by word of mouth while I sat with poets in a park in London, drinking cheap Tesco wine and eating egg salad sandwiches that were probably in the warmest part of my backpack for too long. Carolyn asked if I was open to taking on her daughter as a client, a solemn request tinged with urgency. I excused myself from the group and comforted Carolyn over the phone as she reached a pivotal moment of her own on this journey—the realization that her daughter's time on earth was ending. Misha was going to die. She told me right away that it was pancreatic cancer and they were on the last lap. I knew time wasn't on our side, but I couldn't get back to America for a few days, and she understood.

I hugged everyone I needed to hug in London, and even hopped down to Southampton for a quick frolic and one more hug, then made my way to my home state. Carolyn picked me up from the airport and I made my way to Misha's side, ready to support her in whatever it was she needed from me.

Misha asked if I thought it was important to open a window and let the light in. She read somewhere that spirits have no place to go if all the windows in the room a person dies in are closed. I asked if she planned on dying that day. She laughed again and said no, and we kept them closed. Darkness offers us the opportunity to process thoughts and emotions in ways light can't. Those at the end of their life tend to find that in darkness, there is closure. Additionally, as the body nears the end of its shift, the person transitioning may become more sensitive to the external world. Darkness becomes a companion.

"How are you feeling about dying, Misha?" This simple question, after building a level of trust with the client, opens the door to honest conversations about their fears, hopes, and wishes surrounding the end of their life. I use this question as the jumping-off point with most clients, changing it to "How do you feel about your loved one dying?" when I'm talking to the family and friends of the person who's at the end of their life. It helps to normalize the natural process of dying and foster a sense of acceptance and peace as we move toward the end together. Ultimately this question allows me to acknowledge and honor my clients' feelings about dying so I can empower them to embrace their experience with courage, dignity, and grace.

"How do you feel about dying, Misha?" She adjusted her position a bit so she could stare at the ceiling, where glow-in-the-dark stars had been placed. Their dim glow let me know they were probably there before Misha left this room the first time.

"Let's just get straight to it, huh," Misha asked jokingly, as other clients had. The person actively dying is rarely asked this question by family or friends because that question, to those loved ones, makes death real. Misha said if it weren't for her kids, she'd be ready—that she probably would have died months ago. She didn't think it was fair for kids to lose their mother before their mother could do the big things for them. I asked her what those big things were, and before she answered, I asked if I could write them down. She smiled and nodded.

As Misha began listing the big things she wanted to do for her children, her eyes filled with a wetness that reflected the fading stars. She wanted to be the parent standing up for her daughter when the school called because her daughter was talking way too much in class. She'd miss sitting on sidewalks and eating cotton candy with sticky fingers at parades, like her mom did with her. And she'd miss screaming at the top of her lungs, embarrassing each of her children as they did whatever activity they shamefully invited her to. Misha cried thinking about the prom and how beautiful each of them would look, year after year. "I'm just scared of losing my kids," she said. I grabbed her hand. "I'm just scared of losing my kids before they really know me."

Long before I learned my purpose in this life is to usher light out, I was a writer and storyteller. I still am, even on the days when it pains me to write words, to think of stories to tell—I am these things. I am also a witness to how incredible the universe is when it brings together things and people to make magic.

"This is why I'm here," I said aloud.

"To watch me cry?" Misha asked.

"To help you tell your kids who you are," I said.

I came to sit with Misha six more times, and we found ourselves on a beautiful journey, capturing the essence of who she was and all she wanted to leave behind for her children. By the second visit, we were like family, and we talked to each other as such—deeply and intimately. I asked probing questions: "When was the last time you felt a joy you hoped would never leave you?" "What regrets are weighing you down?"

I'd record her answers in my phone's voice notes and I'd write as much of them as I could simultaneously. When Misha was too tired to talk, she'd make me tell her a story about the world she wanted so badly to see.

I told her about the DJ I fell in love with in Johannesburg and how she would have loved the dances. Misha told me her sense of humor was what she wanted to be remembered for most and shared about the time she superglued her cousin's eyes and mouth shut during a sleepover because her cousin wouldn't let her play whatever video game she was losing on. I told her about the time I was yelled at by a gardener for running through the countless colorful rows of tulips in Hillegom, a town just outside of Amsterdam, but I really wanted a picture surrounded by all that beauty. I'd write her stories while she rested her eyes, and I'd read them to her when they opened. Sometimes I'd hear her snoring and knew it was time for me to leave. I'd go into the living room on my way out, often to find Carolyn sleeping on the couch with tissues surrounding her body and feet. My visits gave respite.

On what I didn't know would be my last visit with Misha,

where we'd talk shit and find things to laugh at, we sat in the quiet stillness of the room after I read Misha's story to her. She was much weaker than she was the first time I visited and my stays were much shorter.

"At least you didn't talk about how small my room was," she said. "Save it for the obituary." She laughed, then I did, too; and we sighed.

For the last time, I asked, "How do you feel about dying, Misha?" With a clarity that belied the weight of her words, she spoke to me about her final moments. She knew there'd be no way to know the moment she'd die, but it was important for her to see her kids as close to the end as possible, to hug and kiss them one last time. She wanted whoever was present to record the audio of her time with them because, if I was telling the truth and hearing is the last thing to go, their voices would be the last thing she'd want to hear. Misha didn't want them in the room when death came. However, she wanted her mother and father holding her hands, but understood if her father wouldn't be able to do it. He had made himself scarce throughout Misha's walk toward death because he couldn't deal with losing his daughter. Misha knew this, and it was important to her that he knew not to feel guilty if he couldn't make it. And if possible, she wanted me there, because even though the room would be even smaller with more people in it, there'd be room for a joke. She said I'd also be there to keep her parents from falling out "like Black folks do every time somebody dies."

"Someone will need to hold them up," she said. Misha asked if it was true that bodily fluids leave the body when we die, and I told her about postmortem purging and how it's simply the body in its final act. She told her mom that before the coroner arrived, someone—anyone—would need to clean her body because she didn't want people talking about how she shat herself. We all laughed that time.

The dress she bought to wear to a party she didn't attend—she'd just been diagnosed a few days prior and was still sinking into her bed—is the dress she wanted to be buried in, even if it was too big now. "It has pockets," she said. I've had many women clients—and even random folks who find out I'm in death work—tell me they're going to put it in writing that they are not to be buried in a bra, and I absolutely understand demanding that justice, but I've never heard of anyone wanting to be buried in a specific outfit because it has pockets.

For Mother's Day, nearly two months after her diagnosis, Misha's children, following her prompt, drew pictures of themselves with their mom on paper with as many crayons as possible. She wanted those pictures folded and put in her pockets "in case we get to take things into heaven," she said.

The last thing Misha told me was about a funeral she'd seen online where the dead man wasn't in a casket but in a chair with a cigarette in his mouth and a bottle of beer in his hand. Someone even lit the cigarette. With a straight face, Misha said this is the kind of funeral she wanted. I looked over to her father, who smiled. He'd come in just before I left. He threw his hands in the air, then threw a hand over his mouth to keep from laughing. Before I could say anything, Misha laughed. It was a joke.

Misha died just a few days after that, with her mother and father holding her hands, listening to the sound of her children singing, talking a lot about nothing, and saying their goodbyes. Carolyn wanted to clean the body alone, and I walked her through it once more before leaving the room with Misha's father. In the darkness of the living room, I did what Misha asked and held her father up.

MY GRANDFATHER, GEORGE WALKER JR.

I WILL FOREVER BE GRATEFUL TO MY PATERNAL grandmother, Irene Elizabeth Jones, for putting thread, needles, scissors, and torn fabrics in my hands as a kid. She'd challenge me to take these mismatched pieces, some barely holding together, and make something. Sometimes I would stare at the tangled threads, wondering what to do next, but she was always there with a knowing look, nudging me to either piece things together or pull them apart and start fresh. Those lessons, taught in a living room on Hardy Drive that felt big as a kid, but now looks small without her in it, were about more than sewing. She was teaching me the art of life—how to mend when things fall apart and when to let go, no matter how hard it is to unravel what we've worked on for so long.

I didn't realize until much later how important those lessons were, how they'd serve me in ways I could never have imagined. Especially when I found myself at my maternal grandfather's bedside, stepping into the role of his death doula. There I realized that life, much like sewing, demands both the skill to mend and the courage to unravel. In those final days with him, I was doing both—stitching together the fragments of his life and unraveling the threads of fear and uncertainty that come with dying.

George Walker Jr. was more than just my mother's father. He was a giant in our family, the kind of man whose presence filled the room even when he wasn't physically there. He makes up a large part of my personality and a small part of my appearance. If it's true what they say and men get their hairline from their mother's father, then this bald look I wear these days is to be blamed on him.

But he was so much more than that. He was the sum of all the stories I'd heard about him, usually in his absence—stories from his old friends, the ones he grew up with in Charlottesville. They'd sit around, reminiscing about their boyhood days, chasing girls and ice-cream trucks, and later, as grown men, chasing bigger things—wives, kids, and sometimes second wives. They'd tell stories about the good old days, the kind that leave you with sore cheeks from laughing too much, and there was always a twinkle in their eyes when they talked about George. He'd say it was a "twinkle of bullshit." His five siblings, too, never missed a chance to tease him when he'd come home for the holidays or birthdays, relishing in memories of the foolishness they all grew up with. My mom and aunt, having been raised right in the middle of all that chaos, could only roll their eyes with affection.

For those of us who see people like him as giants, it's hard to reconcile the idea that they can fall. Giants are supposed to be immortal, or at least live a lot longer than we expect. So when it was time to face his mortality, it felt far too soon, like someone had pressed Fast-Forward on a film we weren't quite ready to be done with.

It all came crashing down on us one afternoon in the hospital. My mom, dad, grandmother, and I were there, waiting for news on whether he could be discharged. He'd been struggling with COPD, and we thought that was the biggest issue. But then the doctor came over, casually asking, "When was the last time he had his colon checked?" I remember thinking, "Why are they asking about his colon if we're here for his lungs?" It felt very much like one of those mechanics trying to upsell you a new air filter when you only came in for an oil change.

While I was busy grumbling about future hospital bills my granddad would feel obligated to pay as the responsible high-credit man he was, my mom whispered something that stuck with me: "I bet it's cancer this time." Sure enough, after a round of tests, waiting, and way too many trips to the hospital cafeteria, we found out it was indeed cancer.

His decline was faster than any of us could have predicted. He went from being the family patriarch, the last of the old guard after his mother passed nearly a decade before, to someone we had to take care of in ways none of us had prepared for. But in those last few months, we found a strange sort of joy amid the sorrow. My grandfather, for all the pain he was in, still had a sharp mind and a sharper sense of humor.

We shared a love of food. He'd suddenly remember a snack he loved as a kid, then ask me if it still existed and where he could get it. I'd find myself driving all over Prince George's County, Maryland, corner store after corner store until I found what he wanted. There were pecan pinwheels, whoopie pies, Junior Mints, and malted milk balls. I'd buy enough for both of us, of course, and we'd sit and share, letting the taste of nostalgia wash over us. These little moments, when we were just eating and laughing together, felt like stolen moments of happiness in the middle of the storm.

There's one Thursday that stands out in my mind. It was just after the cancer diagnosis. We sat at the dining room table with a mountain of Maryland blue crabs between us. He lined up his fork and glass perfectly with the edge of the table before digging in. I watched him do it, thinking about how I'd always done the same, then thinking about how I always thought I was weird because I'd never witnessed anyone else doing it. Turns out, I got it from him. We cracked jokes and crab shells for hours while "In the Heat of the Night" played loudly on the TV in the next room. Time seemed to slow down in those moments. For a brief while, it felt like nothing had changed, like we weren't on the precipice of losing him.

I didn't want that moment to slip away, so I leaned my phone against the napkin holder, recording our conversation. I wanted to capture every word, every laugh. I asked him question after question, trying to make the moment last. He talked about his childhood, the games he played with his brothers, the mischief they got into, including launching pennies at boys who passed by their porch—something I remembered doing with my brother, too. It felt like he was not just passing down stories but pieces of himself, and I was collecting them like treasures.

But life doesn't let us stay in those moments for long. Just days after that beautiful Thursday, everything changed. He couldn't walk anymore. The man who had been cracking jokes and crab legs was now confined to his bed, and with that came a deep sense of shame. It was hard for him to need help, to rely on others for even the most basic things. My grandmother called me into the room one afternoon to help lift him from the bed to the chair while she changed the sheets. As I walked down the hall, I could hear him telling her not to call me, but I kept walking.

When I entered the room, his face said everything he was preparing his mouth to say: "I don't want you to see me like this."

Immediately I responded, "This is what love looks like. Let us love you."

That's when my role shifted. I was no longer just the grandson who fetched his favorite snacks and recorded his stories. I was also his death doula in the truest sense.

It was more than just physical care, though I did plenty of that, too. It was about being there for him emotionally, holding space for him to grieve, to feel the weight of what was happening, and to process it all. Every time I brought him a snack, or we sat down to talk, or I hugged him and told him it was okay to be sad, that was part of the process. It was love, plain and simple.

We had these deep, intimate conversations during that time, especially after my grandmother would finish cleaning him and go to the living room, out of earshot. He'd call me in and tell me to shut the door behind me. Those conversations were just for us, secret spaces where he could unload everything he'd kept hidden from everyone else for over seven decades. He talked about the children he might've fathered, relationships that didn't work out, and the regrets he carried.

There were lighter moments, too. Especially when he'd make me tell him stories from my own life. I told him about the few times I'd had my heart broken, and he'd tell me all the things that must have been wrong with the heartbreakers. I told him about the time I was arrested in a store parking lot after thinking I could outrun store security, and he told me how lucky I was to not be in jail long enough to poop. I told him how much I hated him waking me up early on summer mornings to do chores, even though I loved staying with him. That made him laugh. That also made him call me lazy, making me laugh. And he'd talk about his funeral plans with a sense of humor only someone like him could muster.

"You and I are the smartest in this family," he told me, and I agreed. That was his way of buttering me up to give his eulogy. We planned it all out, knowing that when the time came, it was me who could deliver his energy to the crowd.

In those final days, I couldn't help but reflect on our relationship. We weren't super close when I was younger. He lived too far away for casual visits, so I only saw him on holidays or during family reunions. In my adulthood, I visited more, but not nearly enough—something I know to be true now. As he neared the end, I realized how much we had in common. Some values, the same quirky habits, an adventurous spirit, and a way to make every single thing that ever happened to us fascinating. It felt like in caring for him, I was caring for an older version of myself.

Amid the sorrow and the inevitable end hanging over us like a badly made dream catcher, I found so much gratitude. We had this time together, this precious window to truly connect for the first time, to really get to know each other in a way we hadn't before.

But life, as it always does, had other plans. I had to get back to work, to the life I'd been putting on hold for those last few months. I wasn't there when he died. I was on a plane, waiting to take off, when I got the call. My dad's voice cracked as he told me, and there I was, sitting in the sterile, emotionless airplane cabin, feeling the weight of his words hit me like a ton of bricks as I was told to turn off my phone for takeoff.

There was a brief and immediate moment of sadness. Not for my granddad but for me. I knew there was more for me to learn. But then as I turned off my phone and leaned back in my seat, that sadness melted away, replaced by a deep sense of joy. Joy for the time we'd had and for him knowing I loved him without a doubt. Joy that I'd give his eulogy, just like he'd asked, and that I could honor him in the way he deserved.

While my grandfather is not the one who taught me that life is not about how much time we have but how we use it, he is the one who reminded me. It's about showing up, even when it's hard, even when it's messy.

Just like my grandmother taught me with those tangled threads and mismatched fabrics, life is all about learning how to stitch together the pieces while knowing when to let go and start over. In the end, it's the love we pour into those stitches that holds everything together.

THE MERMAID WHO GREW TIRED OF SWIMMING

AVANTÉ CALLED ME ONE AFTERNOON, HER VOICE as heavy as the July sun we sat under, and the air in her voice was thick. I was sitting on my deck in the middle of the forest, fingers resting on the keyboard, when the phone rang. The name flashed, and for a second I hesitated. Avanté never calls. I knew this was one of those moments.

"Darnell," she said, her voice cracking before she even got the words out. "My mom died."

There was a long silence on the other end of the line. I could hear her breathing. I could feel the weight of what she was about to ask me. I knew before she even said it.

"I need your help," she whispered. "I have to write her obituary."

Now, most people think writing an obituary is just listing facts—birth dates, hometowns, marriages, kids—tidy little paragraphs that sum up an entire existence. The proof is in the bad obituaries I read daily. I read the obituaries in my hometown paper each day, making sure no one I knew died and

I wasn't informed. At most, I spend many hours each week looking through the obituaries from countless cities, towns, and countries, looking for a glimpse into the lives of folks I didn't know but who undoubtedly left their marks on this world. Avanté wanted more than the usual "she was born, she had kids, and she died" obit. Her mom wasn't just another name in the paper. Carolyn was complicated, messy, beautiful, tragic, and Avanté wanted to tell a story that captured that.

At its core, an obituary serves to announce someone's death, but it is also so much more. As someone who sees life nearly everywhere death exists, I see each obituary as an announcement that someone was here. It's a chance for those left behind to honor their dead and share a glimpse of who they were, and to remind the living of the human experience that binds us all. It's a story—often the last one—that we share about someone. And because that is true, shouldn't we strive to make that story as rich and complete as possible?

When I think about Carolyn's obituary, every obituary I've written before hers, and the many I've written since, I consider how little we often know about the people whose lives we summarize. Far too often we compress a lifetime into a paragraph, stripping away the complexities that make a person who they are. Obituaries, in this way, often fail the deceased and those who want to memorialize them. They tell us little more than the fact that someone lived and then died. But what about the *in-between*?

Everyone has a story. Between birth and death, there is a

life—a unique one, filled with moments that shaped a person's existence. If an obituary is the last word on that life, it should be vibrant and reflective of the individual who lived it. This is often the last impression that person will leave on the world. Why not make it one that truly honors their time here?

"She wasn't around much," Avanté said. "But I loved her, Darnell. I did. She wasn't perfect, but she was mine."

In writing obituaries before this one, I've sat across from people, holding their hands as they told me the stories of their loved ones. But this was different. Carolyn hadn't been present in Avanté's life in the way most mothers are. Drugs had stolen years from them. Yet Avanté was determined to honor her mother's memory—not with an obituary that ignored the truth but with one that embraced all of it. The good, the bad, the heartache, and the love.

"What do you remember most about her?" I asked, ready to capture every answer in an attempt to pull blood from a stone.

Avanté laughed softly, and for a moment I could hear a smile in her voice. "Her laugh," she said. "It was contagious. She had this wild sense of humor. And she loved playing with us when she was around. She'd jump out of closets and scare us half to death. But then she'd hug us so tight, like she was afraid to let go."

That was the first note I wrote down: Carolyn had a laugh you'd never forget.

Carolyn Marie Carter. Born in Charlottesville, Virginia, in

1963. Died in the same town in 2022. But those dates? They don't tell you who she was. They don't tell you about the person beneath the surface, about the way her children—Avanté and her brother, Christopher—clung to those small moments they had with her. Moments that flickered like candlelight, brief but bright, lighting up the darkness around them.

Avanté's memories of her mother were scattered, like pieces of a thrift store puzzle that had been lost over time. But the pieces she did have? They were vivid. Carolyn, or "Wilma Durk," as her friends and family called her, was a certified lifeguard—a fact that seemed ironic to Avanté, considering how often her mother had been drowning in her own pain. Carolyn was the kind of person who would give her last dollar to someone who needed it, even when she had nothing left for herself. And when she loved, she loved fiercely.

"She'd push us on the swings," Avanté told me, "underdogging us so high we thought we'd fly right off. Then she'd appear below us, laughing, always laughing. Like a mermaid, just out of reach. She loved mermaids."

But Carolyn wasn't always there. Addiction has a way of stealing people. It wraps itself around them like a riptide, pulling them away from shore before anyone even realizes they're gone, and that's what happened to Carolyn. She slipped away, little by little, until the Carolyn her kids knew became more myth than reality.

Avanté didn't shy away from this truth. She didn't try to paint her mother as something she wasn't. But she also refused to let her mother be defined by her absence. Carolyn had been more than her addiction. She had been a mother, a friend, a woman who loved deeply, even if she didn't always know how to show it.

"She was complicated," Avanté said, her voice steady, "but she was still my mom."

When it came time to write the obituary, I knew the process wouldn't be like the others I had written. It would require me to navigate my way through the lines, pulling beauty from where so much ugliness lived. There were no rainbows in Avanté's retelling of the stories. Carolyn's life was a story—a messy, beautiful, heartbreaking story—and it deserved to be told with all its complexity.

Over and over, I read the notes from my conversation with Avanté and kept typing until the following was complete:

> The words have failed to escape our mouths, so the waters calm themselves enough to speak and tell us about the beautiful, gentle, awful stirring not far below the surface. They tell us about the mermaid who grew too tired to swim. They tell us Carolyn Marie Carter died July 9, 2022. And like all fantastic, tragic, beautiful, wild, and hidden things, she remains a mystery, floating out there just below the surface.
>
> According to the authors, philosophers, and poets, it's the wise ones who are tortured by their minds for lifetimes and we should listen to what it is they are say-

ing even when they are not speaking. We must also listen to the heart. Carolyn's heart is where we find proof that she was not always tortured, but sometimes filled with a love from others that made her heart bigger than her smile. In return, she gave her last to everyone who needed it, even when she wasn't sure how she'd be filled again. This was Carolyn. Named after her dad, Carroll Markelle Carter, she was her father's daughter. This is who the people remember when they talk about her to Joyce Marie Carter, her mother. When they talk to her children, Avanté Carter and Christopher Carter, they tell stories of being cared for and loved by the woman they lovingly called Wilma Durk when they felt the rest of the world turned its back. "She was like a mother to me," they say.

She was a mother and sometimes a myth like UFOs, werewolves, dragons, unicorns, and mermaids. Imperfect and infrequent, but a tight hugger who'd leave kisses all over the faces of her children after jumping out of closets and after pushing them high in swings, underdogging and appearing below like the mermaid she was, with a laugh that will never be forgotten. "She had a crazy sense of humor. I get that from her," Avanté says, remembering better days and holding tight to her mother around Charlottesville, Virginia.

Charlottesville will remember Wilma Durk as the woman who, by example, taught many that life is

> sometimes about doing things for the sole benefit of another. She will be remembered as the woman with not much to give but who still gave all and left this vast sea with nothing but love. And honestly, she'd see that as a beautiful thing.
>
> Carolyn, the certified lifeguard, earned her fins wearing that title proudly. The thing about mermaids is they are survivors in the most dangerous places at all times. Carolyn was a survivor for as long as she could be. The other thing about mermaids, however, is they can still be defeated by their own pain.
>
> Carolyn Marie "Wilma Durk" Carter was fantastic, tragic, beautiful, and wild, and one day, in its own time, the ocean will give her back.

When I finished, I sent it over to Avanté and saved space for her tears, joy, and love. There were no notes, and it went to the printer to be placed in the funeral program. Avanté's family, however, wasn't happy. They wanted more names, more focus on them. But Avanté stood her ground. This wasn't about them. This was about Carolyn. This was about telling her story, not their role in it.

And Carolyn's story? It wasn't simple. It wasn't clean. But it was real.

"Thank you," she said, "for telling her story."

I told her it wasn't me. It was her with the stories, even in pieces, but together they put together a life, and I found a way to write it.

Here's a little not-so-secret: I've already written my obituary. And no, I'm not planning on dying anytime soon! But each year I update it. Sometimes it's just a small addition, like a new milestone or an accomplishment. Other times, it's a complete rewrite. It's a way to make sure that my story—my real story—isn't lost or reduced to a few bullet points in someone's hurried summary of my life. I'm not leaving that to chance.

And neither should you!

Writing your own obituary isn't about being morbid. It's about being intentional. It's about telling the world who you are in your words. And let me tell you, there's power in that. There's a certain freedom in getting to say, "This is who I am. This is how I loved, lived, and struggled. This is the legacy I want to leave behind."

It's also one of the best ways to reflect on your life while you're still living it. What matters most to you? What are the moments, the people, the values that shape who you are?

Trust me, when you start thinking about your life as a story that you get to write, things change. Your choices become clearer. Your priorities shift. Suddenly the everyday grind doesn't seem as important, and what does matter rises to the surface.

So here's my challenge to you: Take the time to write

your obituary. Don't wait for someone else to tell your story. Start today. Tell your story in your words. And if it changes tomorrow, update it. Let it evolve with you, because your life is constantly growing, shifting, and deepening with each experience.

You might think you're not ready or that your story isn't "big" enough yet. But trust me, every life—your life—has beauty, complexity, and significance. The only person who can truly capture that? You.

So grab a pen or open up a blank document and start writing. Tell the world about the life you've lived and the one you're still building. Own your narrative. Share the moments that matter. Celebrate your achievements and reflect on your challenges. And as you grow, keep adding to it. Keep refining it.

The best part? When it's all said and done, you'll have written a love letter to the life you lived—a letter that no one else can write for you.

Take it from someone who does this often—this process isn't just for when you're gone. It's a gift to yourself while you're here.

DANNY

DANNY FOUND ME A FEW WEEKS AFTER HIS TERMINAL diagnosis and asked if I'd ever been to Seattle. I remember hearing how surprised he was when I shared that I lived in Seattle for a year in my mid-twenties but left after realizing that seasonal depression, for me, extended well beyond its normal seasons, and I felt too young to be there. He asked if I'd return to Seattle to help him with, as he called it, "death stuff." Within a week, I was sitting across from him in one of the many coffee shops the city boasts, drinking a chai latte because coffee makes me shake. We talked about how we'd go about getting his family to give him the funeral he wanted, not the one they insisted he have.

Danny was raised in a Christian household and married a Christian woman. So, when he came to terms with his coming death and shared the news with his wife, mother, and children, they almost immediately began discussing a Christian funeral. There would be a wake, a funeral service held in a church, and a burial as close to his father's grave as possible. There would be hymns, prayers, and eulogies where they'd emphasize the belief in the Resurrection and eternal life throughout. Danny, however, had been Muslim for seven years and he wanted to die and his body be treated as such.

When Muslims die, there are several traditions and rituals. Danny hoped for a transition that allowed him to be aware enough to sense when the end was near so the last words from his mouth would be the Shahada, a declaration of faith stating "I bear witness that there is no god but Allah, and Muhammad is the messenger of Allah." It was important to him to affirm his faith as he transitioned to death.

Upon death, he wanted the men from his mosque, the men he called "brother," to perform *ghusl*. They would wash Danny's body three times with the utmost respect, in a manner that preserved Danny's dignity and modesty.

After the ghusl, Danny's body would be shrouded in a simple white cloth called a *kafan*. "The simpler the better," Danny said. The simplicity of the shroud is to remind everyone that worldly possessions and status are left behind and that there is an equality that comes with death.

Following the shrouding of Danny's body, Salat al-Janazah, the prayer service, would be performed. This prayer service would be brief and held in an open space so the family who aren't Muslim would feel comfortable attending. Danny told me this prayer is unique in that it is silent, and those in attendance pray for the mercy and forgiveness of the deceased.

"There's no need to keep my body around for weeks like

they did my father," Danny said. His burial, as is tradition in his faith, would be done as soon as possible after death. His body would be placed in a simple grave, without a casket, and positioned on its right side facing Mecca, the holy city. On his grave he wanted a simple marker to also symbolize equality in death.

This is everything Danny wanted, but his family struggled to accept the little he told them regarding the matter, holding on to their Christian beliefs and customs, unwavering. Danny had no clue how to approach the matter without breaking hearts or instigating drama. It was a conflict that brought to the surface the complexities of faith, identity, and family loyalty, leaving Danny in a difficult position as he faced the end of his life. It was the conflict that brought me to Seattle.

Working with Danny to help him advocate for his wishes became a delicate and deeply personal journey. I began by sharing stories of others I had worked with—like Mill, whose family honored her wish for a quiet, natural burial in the woods she loved. The years and the seconds leading her to her death were peaceful because she knew that every detail had been arranged according to her desires, and she knew she could fully trust the people in place to see that these desires became a reality. On the other hand, I told Danny about Cliff, a man who hadn't made his wishes clear before he lost the ability to communicate. His family members, completely unsure of what he would have wanted, argued bitterly over how to handle his funeral, leading to a service that left everyone feeling regretful and unsettled. A service I know Cliff would have hated to see.

In the event that Danny would no longer be able to communicate his medical and end-of-life wishes at some point, and understanding early on in my visit that he came from a family that may not want to do as he suggests, I told him about the importance of documenting his wishes in legal documents such as a living will and an advance directive. We spent a lot of time in the first couple of days together going over these documents, discussing pain relief, breathing tubes, blood transfusions, ventilators, and more. First, it was just the two of us, then Danny invited his youngest child, his daughter Kelly, to join us. As sad as she was throughout the discussions of her father's health and eventual death, she was glad everything was in place to protect his choices if he could no longer speak for himself, and she was relieved she wouldn't have to be the one going against the family alone.

Kelly was open to listening. When she was around, she and I would sit with Danny, discussing his wishes in detail and listening to the stories she'd never heard about her father as a kid. I validated Kelly's feelings, acknowledging how difficult it must be to reconcile her love for her father with the reality of his impending death. Yet I reassured her that by helping Danny plan, she was not only honoring his wishes but also relieving herself and the rest of the family from making painful decisions later on. Kelly became an essential ally in communicating Danny's wishes to the rest of the family and even to his doctors and the religious leaders who would be involved in his final rites. Together we ensured that, at the very least, Danny's voice would be heard. Danny made Kelly his health-care proxy but ensured her he'd do his best to not add any additional stress to her life, and she'd likely only remain that in name, not action.

With Danny leading the charge, and Kelly and myself as backup, Danny's family finally came around to understanding his desire for a death and funeral that respected his faith. It wasn't easy. Years of Christian upbringing and traditions were deeply ingrained in his wife, mother, and other children. But with time, compassion, and Danny's patient explanations of what his Muslim faith meant to him, they began to see the importance of honoring his wishes. Danny and I were able to spend the remainder of my time with him in Seattle finding unique ways to tell the stories he wanted to leave behind for whoever wanted to read them. He was still very much alive, active, and present, so much so that I often forgot why I was even there. We laughed, reminisced, and even debated what stories were worth telling and which should be left untold. I'm always on the side of "Tell all the stories you possibly can," but I also understand why many of my clients want to leave out parts of their lives.

Danny seemed so full of life that it was easy to forget he was dying. But just weeks after I left Seattle, I received the call from Danny's son, telling me that Danny died, and he invited me to the funeral. Hesitantly I asked when it would be, and he told me it was going to be held in a little over a week and a half in Tacoma. My heart broke a little, assuming—but truly knowing—that meant Danny would not be getting the Muslim funeral he'd hoped for.

When I arrived at the funeral, it was indeed the Christian ceremony that Danny didn't want. The church was filled with the sounds of hymns, prayers, and eulogies. Danny's body was laid out in a casket, surrounded by flowers, and his family spoke of his Christian upbringing, focusing on the belief in the Resurrection and eternal life. I sat quietly in the back, trying to avoid having to talk to Danny's family. Before leaving the church, I was stopped by a couple of the brothers from the mosque who were just as saddened by the decision to ignore Danny's wishes as I was. But there was a speck of light they were able to offer.

They told me that Danny, in the end, was fully aware and knew the end was coming. The last words from his mouth, over and over, were the Shahada. Thanks to Danny's daughter, his youngest child, who understood the importance of listening and allowing people to live and die on their own terms, the brothers from the mosque were called to the house. They washed his body properly, shrouded him in three pieces of cloth, and after wrapping Danny, they performed Salat al-Janazah. Sadly, that is where Danny's wishes ended.

"But at least he had that," one of the brothers said.

"He deserved more," I replied, feeling the weight of those words.

In death, as in life, people deserve to have their wishes respected. It is a final act of dignity and honor, a way to let them leave this world on their own terms, surrounded by the beliefs and traditions they held dear. Those who are in charge of making these decisions must listen, not only because it's what the deceased wanted but also because it's a reflection of the respect we all owe each other in life and in death. Danny may not have had the full Muslim funeral he desired, but in his final moments, he clung to the words that meant the most to him. Thanks to his daughter, he was granted a small piece of what he wanted. It wasn't everything, but it was something. And sometimes that something is all we have.

NEAL

THE NIGHT NEAL POPPED UP IN MY DMS, I WAS HALF asleep, wondering why I hadn't already shut down my phone and computer for the night. The message was concise but firm, the kind of tone that left no room for delay: "Can I call you now? It's kind of important."

I gave him my number and when he called, I could hear the weariness in his voice. It wasn't the kind of exhaustion that comes after a long day, but a long life—when carrying the weight of it all has left your body too tired to breathe. He didn't say much at first. His voice was more of a whispered confession, a release into the air that tonight might be the night he would leave.

Neal shared something he hadn't told anyone. He'd been diagnosed with a disease he was certain he couldn't live with. He had watched others suffer with the same diagnosis, and many of them had died—some in ways that left permanent, ugly scars on his mind. Neal described the fear he felt in his bones, not just from the disease itself but from the slow decline he was convinced awaited. The thought of withering away, of losing pieces of himself, was too much.

"I'm not sure what made me reach out to you," he said, "but something told me I had to." At this time, we'd been Facebook friends for months or years or perhaps just a few days, but we had never spoken. Social media is strange that way.

In that moment I recognized how powerful it was for Neal to honor that whisper inside him, because sometimes it's all we have. That tiny voice, almost drowned by despair, was telling him there was still something left to explore. A death doula's role is not only about preparing for the immediate end but also walking someone through their darkest hours, helping them see the paths they can take, even when they feel like all options have closed.

Neal didn't contact me because he wanted a pep talk. He didn't need someone to convince him to hold on for one more day. He called because in the midst of his sadness, he wanted what we all want in those moments—to feel seen. He wanted to feel understood, and maybe, more than anything, he wanted to feel that if tonight were truly his last, he didn't have to be lonely.

Neal reached out because of my relationship with death, hoping the work I do was for not just the terminally ill or elderly but anyone on the edge of life and death, navigating that fragile space where darkness feels endless and tomorrow feels optional.

Being a death doula for Neal and others who carry such weight doesn't mean I stop them from feeling what they're feeling. It's not my job to talk someone off the ledge, to force optimism on a heart that's already decided it's had enough. My role is to sit in that moment with them, to offer them something I wish more people received when life becomes unbearable: compassionate, nonjudgmental presence.

When Neal reached out, he needed to know that it was okay to speak his truth. His truth in that moment was that he was ready to let go. But part of him wanted to make sure that, if he did, someone would witness his pain, honor his journey, and understand that this choice wasn't about giving up but seeking peace. I gave him that space, and that's what death doulas offer—a space for honesty, without the pressure to fix, heal, or change anything. We walk beside those who are nearing the end of their journey, not only when the cause is "natural."

For Neal, having a death doula meant having someone who wouldn't judge him for how he felt. I could sit with him through the darkness and help him navigate options, holding his truth as sacred, regardless of what it looked like. We talked that night, and as I listened, I also gave him what death doulas give so many: permission—not permission to die, but permission to feel what he was feeling, to explore his thoughts fully and openly without fear of being shamed. I also reminded him that there was no rush, that even in his despair, time was still his, and he could choose to take as long as he needed.

In those moments, Neal told me, he was able to think through his pain in a way he hadn't allowed himself to before. There was no pressure to make any decisions; just an invitation to reflect, to be present with his feelings, and to know that no matter what, he wasn't alone. My job as a death doula is to guide, to hold space, and to help a person explore the full spectrum of their choices—life, death, and everything in between.

For those who are suicidal, having a death doula can be invaluable. We are not therapists, but we are trained to walk with people through the most challenging transitions. A death doula can also help create ritual. Rituals can take many forms, and they can help anchor someone like Neal in the present moment instead of wandering to a future self that's frightening. A ritual is an intentional act—something done with purpose and heart—that's meant to bring a sense of comfort, connection, or grounding, especially when the ground beneath us feels unsteady. For Neal, one example of this could be creating a morning practice where he lights a candle to honor both the life he's living and those he's lost. It could be as simple as taking a few minutes each day to breathe deeply while listening to a favorite song or the birds or the water babbling nearby, reminding him of the beauty that still exists. Another ritual might be writing a letter to himself at the end of each day, highlighting both the struggles and victories, which allows him to reflect on the fact that he's still here, still choosing life, even when it's hard. These rituals act as small but powerful reminders that life, even in its most difficult moments, is still worth honoring.

That night with Neal wasn't about saving a life—it was about honoring one. It was about showing him that even in his most desperate moments, there was room for grace, compassion, and the small hope that maybe, just maybe, tomorrow could look different.

That night was years ago, and Neal and I have stayed in touch. Our relationship, which began in the depths of his despair, has evolved into something more—a partnership in navigating life's hardest truths. There are still days where the weight of his diagnosis presses down on him, when old fears resurface and hope seems like a distant memory. There are more good days; days where Neal finds pockets of joy, when he remembers that life, even with its uncertainties, still has moments worth holding on to.

When the bad days come, Neal will call. He's open about where his mind goes in those moments, and I have come to expect that in his vulnerability, there's also a request for clarity. He doesn't just need someone to listen; he needs to know I'm prepared for what might come. He'll tell me, "If you wake up to a message from my mom that I'm dead, you know what to do. I want you to know I tried, but it was just too much." Those conversations are hard, but they are also part of the journey, part of the truth Neal carries with him. My job isn't to make him promises about things I can't control but to honor his wishes.

Each time we talk and the conversation is hard, heavy, and dark, I remind Neal that he still has a choice—one he gets to make on his terms. Whether that choice leads him toward more good days or a final decision to end his suffering, my role is to stand beside him, to honor his life while he's here, and to respect the legacy he chooses to leave behind. That's the sacred work of a death doula—holding space for both life and death, and knowing that sometimes the two are more intertwined than we ever imagined.

In this work, I help people see that death, much like life, can be a deeply personal and sacred experience. Sometimes, in holding space for someone's potential death, I inadvertently provide the tools to keep living. Being a death doula is being a life doula.

For those who are suicidal, having a death doula isn't about making decisions for them. It's about standing with them, offering a light in the darkness, and reminding them that they are still in control of their story, whether that story ends tonight or continues another day. In that first conversation with Neal, I wasn't just his death doula. I became a witness to his pain, and in the end, I became a witness to his choice to live.

SELF-CARE

THIS WORK IS HEAVY, LAYERED WITH THE EMOTIONAL toll that comes from witnessing the end of life up close and being a caregiver for those who are dying. I've learned that to truly hold space for others, I must first hold space for myself. When I talk about the work I watched my grandmother, mother, and many others do, I do so while remembering that "holding space" wasn't a concept they heard repeatedly, and even if they did, it wasn't something they had the time and resources to embrace. For me, prioritizing self-care is nonnegotiable. The stress, anxiety, sadness, and weight of this role don't simply disappear after I leave a client's bedside. Those emotions linger like the perfume families often smell in the house long after their loved ones have departed. It's imperative to not only acknowledge these feelings but also actively address them. If I don't take care of myself, I can't be fully present for those who need me most.

Self-care is more than just a buzzword we see every time we log on to social media or hear in spas, in massage parlors, in nail salons, or on beaches—it's a necessity for everyone who's able. It's the practice of listening to our inner compass, finding what keeps us steady and grounded, especially when life feels heavy and unpredictable. For caregivers, the intensity of the demands on our giving can make it feel like we're inside a sealed vault that's quickly running out of air. But self-care isn't only for those people in caregiving roles. It's for anyone who's ever felt the strain of life, shouldered grief, stress, or experienced the general exhaustion of simply being human. Self-care is about reclaiming that vault and pumping more air into it. It's about filling ourselves back up so we can continue giving to ourselves and those we choose to serve. Without it, the burnout we work hard to keep at bay is inevitable, and the ability to truly be present, for both life's highs and lows, dies.

One of the questions I ask my clients, whether they're nearing the end of their life or freshly navigating the weight of grief, is, "How do you take care of yourself?" The only time I'm disappointed by the answers is when they tell me they don't, and I immediately jump into "Let's get you cared for" mode. But there have been many clients who show me that there are endless ways to nurture our spirits and pull joy into ourselves. Sometimes their self-care routines are so incredible that I adopt them for myself. After Jared passed, for instance, I started going to estate sales on the weekends. Jared loved hunting for unique treasures, and it was a form of joy that grounded him. I thought, "Why not give it a try?" Now I find myself searching for hidden gems in stranger's houses and yards when I have Saturdays and Sundays free—letting the thrill of discovery lift me up. It's a small, beautiful way to stay connected to life, and it has become part of my self-care practice.

I was a faithful fan of the show *Parks and Recreation*, and I remember when Donna and Tom introduced us to "Treat Yo' Self Day." It's a day to celebrate yourself, but also to show yourself some much-needed appreciation by treating yourself to the luxuries you've been neglecting for a while. When I'm talking and building community with other death doulas, caregivers, and people who give so much of themselves, I do not hesitate to remind them to remember to take care of themselves. For me, that self-care looks like road trips, exploring new places, cooking, journaling, spending time with people who bring me joy, walking, and thousands of other things that make my face light up. For others, it could be as simple as finding a moment of quiet or as unique as watching ants build entire towns, highways, and byways out of dirt. No matter what it looks like, self-care is an essential reminder that we all deserve to feel whole.

When I worked with Hiram, a man who approached his death much like he approached his life—with his knife out, ready to take down anyone who stood in the way of him doing it his own way—I could feel the weight of his grief for the life he was leaving behind. After spending long days with him, ensuring he felt seen and heard, I found myself carrying his sadness on my back, in the place where my stress is usually stored. To release it, I traveled to South Africa, then Morocco, then Spain. Hiram wanted to see far more of the world than he actually saw, and his passing reminded me that there is so much I've yet to see. Traveling allows me to reconnect with life when I've been steeped in death. My first stop was Durban, where I stood ankle-deep in the ocean while the waves helped me feel grounded again, filling me up with a fresh energy needed to continue in death work.

Jasmine's passing hit me differently. She was a mother, and the grief of her young children weighed heavily on me. I knew that once I left her family's side after the funeral, I needed something to bring me back to a space of joy. That's when I turned to the brand-new standing mixer, blender, zester, and chopping block in my kitchen. I found new recipes that excited me and gave me something to look forward to. Thinking of Jasmine and her love for mac and cheese and feeding friends, I invited a few friends over for a dinner party and tried out a recipe I had been contemplating for weeks. Preparing foods, sharing a meal, laughing, and creating something beautiful out of fresh ingredients always reminds me that life continues, even in the face of loss. This would explain why the repast is arguably the most important part of a funeral.

Gloria, a woman who fought until her last breath, showed me resilience I had never witnessed. When I finished my work with her, I found myself full of thoughts and emotions that needed a place to go. I have what feels like hundreds of journals where my thoughts are scattered. I turned to them, as I often do, and let it all out. For at least ten minutes every day, I write. I don't judge the words; I don't worry about grammar or structure. I just let whatever's inside come out. The day after Gloria died, those ten minutes turned into thirty, then an hour, until I had written myself into peace again.

Sylvester's humor kept me laughing even as he said his final goodbyes, but that laughter didn't erase the ache of watching him leave. After his death I needed to be surrounded by people who bring me joy, the ones who remind me what it feels like to be alive and all the things I can do with this life. I spent time with close friends, letting their lightness lift the heaviness I was feeling. Whether we're dining out or sitting at home flipping through a streaming service for hours in hopes of finding something funny or extremely dramatic, talking about nothing and everything, being with them brings me back to who I want to show up as in this world.

Finally, I walk. It's simple, but walking brings me back to my body after I've spent so much time focusing on others. After Sylvester's passing, I went for a long walk, letting the sounds of nature remind me that there is still life all around me. The rhythm of my feet on the ground helps me process what I've seen, heard, and felt. It gives me space to breathe.

This work is not easy, but I am committed to it because I don't know how not to do it. It's who I am. But I also know that if I don't care for myself, I can't do this work well.

If you are a caregiver, please do not allow yourself to burn out. I know it can be difficult—it's hard to trust that someone will take care of your loved ones just as good as you do—but you must trust that.

Take care of yourself.

LETTA AND ETHAN

LETTA AND ETHAN WERE A DYNAMIC COUPLE IN their forties who seemed to have everything figured out, and had since their mid-twenties. They met during their freshman year in college and made the relationship official the summer before their senior year. They had thriving careers. Letta was an environmental engineer hoping to make the planet a little bit better than she found it, and Ethan was an elementary school teacher trying to not become jaded by the education system. They had three beautiful children, a dog, a chicken coop out back, and a love that was palpable even through the phone. They were healthy, happy, and, as they claimed, in the best shape of their lives. It wasn't a crisis or a health scare that brought them to me; it was something far more deliberate. They wanted to plan for the inevitable, even though it seemed so far away.

I made it to their home just in time for plenty of eggs, potatoes, and avocado toast. "How would you like to die?" I asked, just as I ask each client who is at the end of their life. This question is for everyone.

"We want to die having done something our parents never did for us," Letta said.

Ethan nodded in agreement, chasing his eggs with a matcha latte.

Letta continued: "Planning. We want to make sure everything is in place for our kids. We don't want them to have to go through what we did with our families."

We took a moment to honor the fact that we were all part of a generation attempting to break bad habits.

Their story wasn't unique to me. In fact, most times when I arrive to meet a new client, there is no paperwork and no plan other than dying. What was unique to Letta and Ethan was their intention. They were proactive, determined to spare their children the confusion and chaos they'd experienced as young adults because their parents had no plans for their deaths or the immediate after. Due to cancer, an accident, and suicide, Ethan and Letta moved through the world without parents. They wanted to create a road map, not just for their deaths but also the aftermath their children would face. As parents and providers, they wanted to leave behind clarity instead of questions. A plan instead of panic.

We put away the dishes, pulled out our laptops, notepads, document templates, pens, pencils, and snacks to get us through, and we got to work. When you're staring at so much paper, so many empty lines, a list of endless questions, it can feel like you're deep in the bushes with no sunlight coming through. As we fought our way out of the bushes, our pens and pencils and keystrokes like machetes, Letta and Ethan began to share stories about their families. It was almost as if each topic we covered opened a floodgate of memories, each one tied to an untimely or unplanned death in their family.

Letta's mother had been in an awful car accident and hospitalized with life-threatening injuries. She was only fifty-four with no plans in place. Letta, with her voice catching, painted a picture of her mother for me. She was the one in the family who had it all together—a job, a home, kids who made her look good. Everyone leaned on her when they were in trouble, and she never turned them away. But when she was gone, everything and every place felt empty and there were more questions than answers. "We had no idea what she would have wanted," Letta said.

Letta and her siblings were left to deal with the chaos that comes with sickness and death, trying to make decisions about their mother's care in her final days and, later, her funeral and burial.

"There were arguments and hurt feelings because none of us knew what she wanted. We were all guessing, trying to honor her but really just projecting our own needs and desires," Letta said.

This is what many families end up doing. Long before calling myself a death doula, I watched over and over how sickness and death brought out the pettiness of others, and how those petty people did whatever they could to craft what they felt the dying or deceased person should have.

Ethan's story wasn't too different. His father had been a larger-than-life figure, a man who took pride in building his home and business from the ground up. He was meticulous in his work but never once spoke about what he wanted in death. When he was diagnosed with a terminal illness, it was as if he was determined to pretend it wasn't happening.

"He just wouldn't talk about it," Ethan said. "Even when it was clear he didn't have much time left, he would change the subject. Every decision we made was behind his back."

I've helped many families plan deaths and funerals for their loved ones that felt more like we were planning surprise parties. It was always in secret, always whispers, and doing our best to keep the one dying in the dark.

Ethan's father died in hospice, and though many decisions were already made by his family without his knowledge, there were many left to make: cremation or burial, a church funeral or just something by the graveside.

"It felt like we were doing him a disservice," Ethan said. "But he never gave us the chance to do it right."

Letta and Ethan were determined not to leave their children in the same situation. As we sat together, hour after hour, downing fruit snacks, applesauce cups, and cookies, we tackled each element of the end-of-life planning with a determination that was both inspiring and humbling. I guided the ship as they approached it all like a business meeting, complete with bullet points and follow-up questions. But there was a tenderness to it, too, a deep abiding love for each other and their children.

We started with their advance directives. They wanted to be clear about their wishes if they were ever in a position where they couldn't speak for themselves. Ethan, who'd been notably laid-back and easygoing since our first meeting, became intensely serious as we discussed this. "I don't want to be kept alive if there's no quality of life," he said as soon as we began. "I've seen too many people just . . . existing. I don't want that."

Letta agreed, smirking while telling Ethan she'd gladly pull the plug, should the time come. She told him she wanted nearly the same, but there were a few nuances to her request. She wanted to make sure that if there was any chance of recovery, her family would hold on, but she also didn't want them to suffer through a long, drawn-out process. "I want to live, really live, until I can't anymore," she said. "But I don't want to be a burden."

They chose health-care proxies outside of each other. Letta chose her baby sister because she knew she'd fight to the death for what Letta wanted. Ethan chose his fraternity brother, a man he said he's been to hell and back with and could trust with everything he's ever loved. These two people are who they trusted to carry out their wishes without hesitation. It was an emotional moment, watching them think through these decisions, and we needed a break for lunch.

The funerals were next. I let them know that, like the proxies, these plans could be changed at any time. I told them about my own plans and how they change nearly every time I hear a new song I love or walk into an incredible space. That helped ease the pressure they felt going into the conversation, and they approached it with a surprising amount of humor and grace.

"I want it to be a party," Letta said, laughing. Funny enough, more times than not, that's exactly what my clients want. My friends, too. There's something about people eating, drinking, being merry, and telling stories over breakbeats that feels good to us. Perhaps it helps us to know we didn't bring too much sadness to people, or at least we want to break it up with a moment of joy.

They both chose to be cremated, a decision that felt right to them. Ethan wanted his ashes buried at the foot of his mother's grave. Letta wanted her ashes separated and scattered in her favorite places. Some would be spread in New Orleans, some on a beach in Curaçao, and some in the garden just outside their back door. "This is where my kids can sit with me," she said. "It's peaceful there," Ethan said.

They planned the details of their services with the same care they put into everything else. Letta wanted sunflowers and a live band playing her favorite gospel songs, including "Trouble of the World," to be sung just like Mahalia Jackson did in *Imitation of Life*, a movie Letta and her mother watched countless times. Ethan wanted a barbecue with a gathering of all his friends, fraternity brothers, and family, sharing stories and laughing. "I want it to feel like I'm there, still part of the party," he said.

While etching out each part of their plan, the stories of their family members who hadn't planned came tumbling out. Letta's uncle had died suddenly, leaving behind a mess of financial and legal issues. "He had money," Letta said, shaking her head. "But no will, no instructions. His kids ended up in court, fighting over everything. It was ugly."

Her great-aunt, a woman she'd always called the most organized person in her life, had a plan for everything in her life, but nothing for her death. She'd simply say, "Y'all will figure it out."

Ethan's grandmother had been a pillar of strength in his family, but when she passed, it became clear that no one knew what to do. "She never talked about it," he said. "She was old-school, you know? Death wasn't something you planned for. It was just something that happened. But it left us all messed up."

Each story was a testament to the pain and confusion that can follow a death without plans. It wasn't just about the logistics, though those were hard enough. It was the emotional toll of not knowing, of having to make decisions in the midst of grief, of feeling like you were failing someone you loved.

Another break, another snack, and a good stretch, followed by a meditation Ethan pulled up on his phone. We sat quiet, took some deep breaths, and listened as the guide helped us release some tension we'd built up over the last hours, caused by family members who weren't even there. By the time we finished their plans, Letta and Ethan had created something truly beautiful. It was more than just a set of instructions for their children. It was a gift of peace and clarity. Those, too, are love. They had thought through every detail, from who would care for their children if something happened to both of them much sooner than expected, to how they wanted their estates handled, to the words they wanted spoken at their services.

They left nothing to chance, and in doing so, they created a legacy that went far beyond anything material. They were giving their children and loved ones the freedom to grieve without the added burden of uncertainty.

We finished dinner and they finished writing rough drafts of their obituaries. We pushed our way through dessert, then drank tea while laughing at how much dysfunction our families have in common when it comes to leaving every decision we should make to those left behind. When we finally wrapped up our sessions, there was a sense of completion, of something deeply right having been done.

"I feel lighter," Letta said, smiling. "Like we've taken care of something really important."

Ethan said he felt like a survivor, having worked on these plans for more than ten hours.

"It is a relief, though," Ethan said, "knowing our kids won't have to worry about it. That they can just . . . remember us."

We gave grace to those generations before us who didn't do the work, because many of them weren't afforded access to the resources or the time to plan.

As a death doula, I often see the worst of what happens when these conversations don't happen. I see families torn apart by disagreements, people paralyzed by the fear of making the wrong choice, loved ones drowning in guilt and regret. But Letta and Ethan were reminders of what's possible when we face these things head-on.

They weren't just planning for their deaths but also for their lives—for the way they would be remembered and the legacy they would leave behind. They were, in every sense, living proof that preparing for the end isn't about death at all. It's about love. It's about the people we leave behind and the peace we give them.

In helping Letta and Ethan, I was reminded of one of the reasons I do this work. It's not about death. It's about life—the lives we touch, the memories we leave, the love we pass on. It's about making sure that when we're gone, the people we love have everything they need to carry on, not just with our memories but with the certainty that we cared enough to plan. It's about writing the final chapter of our story in a way that honors every chapter that came before it.

LIFE DOULA

PEOPLE OFTEN ASSUME MY WORK IS SOLELY ABOUT the end—about guiding people through their final days, hours, and minutes as compassionately as I know how, often raising hell inside hospitals. While that's true, it's only part of the story. Yes, I help people prepare for the end of life they want, assist them in telling their stories, and provide support as they transition. But there's another, often overlooked aspect of this work: helping people truly live in the days they have left. In those moments, when time is simultaneously finite and infinite, I've seen folks embrace life more fully than ever before. I make no apologies for being an enabler of that. And some of my clients have shown me just how interconnected life and death really are.

Isaac was an old-fashioned man—but young enough to be my older brother—who had lived a life filled with practicality and responsibility. He grew up with a father who stressed the importance of settling down with a woman who'd give him children and working the same job until retirement. After a few years of trimming the hedges, road trips to see the grandkids, and finally getting that luxury car he always dreamed of, he could die. It was a life, and Isaac bought into it. He became an engineer solely for the salary, knowing it would provide a life for himself and the wife he'd one day find. Two years after finding her, they had twin boys, and Isaac worked harder, unfulfilled. What wasn't in his dad's wishful plans was sickness. At forty-five, Isaac learned he'd never reach retirement or get that luxury car or trim any hedges or see any grandchildren that may come. In his last days, Isaac expressed two of his deepest regrets: he did everything to please his parents—mostly his father; and he never became the painter he'd always wanted to be.

"I haven't picked up a brush since sixth grade," he told me. He had spent his life admiring art from a distance, always telling himself, "One day." He figured at a minimum, that would be part of his retirement plan.

I remember sitting beside him, listening to the sadness in his voice and feeling that ache that comes from knowing a dream will go unexplored. But I also felt something else as I looked around that hospice room—a spark of possibility. I told him what I tell folks often—that as long as there was breath in his body, it isn't too late. If he wanted to be a painter, then we would make him a painter, and I pointed to the walls, telling him we'd make his final place a museum.

The next day I brought canvases, brushes, and an assortment of paints. Isaac's eyes lit up like a child seeing a toy store for the first time. The hospice nurses were just as happy, agreeing that a place filled with so much death should have more color and life. He was hesitant at first, his hands shaking slightly as he picked up a brush, mostly from the slight pain as he waited for the medicine to kick in.

"What if I'm no good?" he asked, and I could see the fear of failing at something he'd built up in his mind for so long. I told him what I tell all artists—that it wasn't his job to wonder if he was good or not. His job was to create the thing he was moved to create, so the world can have it. Nothing else mattered but the joy felt when creating it.

He dipped his brush into a pool of cerulean blue and made his first stroke. Then another, and another. I watched the lines and figures form on the canvas, then watched his face transform as he painted, the pain seeming to peel away as he immersed himself in art. It was as if he was painting his life onto the canvas, all the emotions and experiences he'd kept bottled up flowing out in hues of blue, green, and yellow.

I wasn't with Isaac until the end, but I was there long enough to see him become the painter he'd always wanted to be. We hung three of his paintings on the wall before I left, and his wife later told me he completed several more pieces that now hang on the walls in several homes, one being the home of his parents. She said when he died, he did so with a peace she realized she'd never seen in him. In helping him become a painter, I helped him live.

I remember Silvia and the call I got from her the day she refused more treatment. "I'm done," she said, her voice calm.

"If I'm going to die, I want to die an adventurer." This was our first conversation. Silvia had been a homebody for most of her life, never straying far from her small town. She told me once how she believed that we all get a certain number of lives and we can tell if we are nearing the end of our supply or if we have many more ahead of us. She said she was new, fresh out of the box, because she wasn't quick to take risks, she held on tightly to material things, and she never moved far from home. I joked that I must be in my last. But now, for Silvia as she stared down death, there was a sense of urgency to experience the world in a way she never had before, as though that life would be her last.

The night before learning further treatment would only get her a few miserable months, Silvia had a dream that made her want to backpack through Asia. She'd never been, never even had a passport, but she was sure of Asia. In college, she'd won a scholarship to travel through Europe for the summer, but as she stood in line to get her passport photo, fear of the unknown crippled her and she canceled everything. Although she had always wondered what incredible things would have happened had she gone, she put off other potential experiences for the same reason, and for reasons most of us understand: work, family, fear of a little discomfort.

Death has a way of clearing away any power those reasons hold over us. Silvia was ready to go, and she called me to help make it happen. After hearing I was a death doula and writer, she searched for more information on me to see if we'd be a match, and she found that travel is one of my favorite things.

After talking every day for a week about her tastes, fears, lodging requirements, and abilities, I booked Silvia a two-week trip that started in Hong Kong and ended in Seoul. I bought her the first journal she'd ever owned, encouraging her to document her journey not just in words but also in feelings. I wanted her to capture the scent of the street food, the texture of the temples, the laughter of the people she'd meet. And she did. Silvia sent me photos of herself standing in front of a sidewalk food stand, eating what looked like a whole fried frog in Kuala Lumpur; bathing in a tub filled with flowers in Bali; and sitting at a bar, toasting mocktails with a bartender in Piss Alley, Tokyo, with a sign next to her that said "No photos inside." Each photo radiated with a kind of joy that transcended her circumstances.

In an email she told me about the people she met along the way—other travelers who were surprised, and some inspired, by her story. When Silvia passed away, she did so as the adventurer she always wanted to be, her journal filled with the stories of her last great journey. She sent me photos of a few pages from her journal. "I thought I was dying," she wrote, "but I think I've never felt more alive."

Audrey's story is a little different, and it's the one that sticks with me the most—in ways I dislike. She called me between the day she was told just how bad her heart was and the surgery that would hopefully save her life. The doctors were clear—the surgery had a low survival rate, but without it, she would definitely die. Audrey was convinced that if she didn't die before the surgery, she'd definitely die in surgery. So she called me not to help her prepare for death but to help her do a lot of living before death found her. She'd read something I'd written about my blood-clotting condition and how I was told I could die at any given moment, but I've never let it stop me—sometimes foolishly—from living the life I want.

"I don't want to waste any more time," she said.

The enabler in me was ready to lend a hand in whatever she had up her sleeves. "What do you want to do?" I asked.

"I want to quit my job," she said, her voice cracking. "I hate it. I've always hated it."

I encouraged her to do just that—to walk away from what never served her, if she could afford to. And she did. Then her list of what she wanted to do got longer.

With her newfound freedom, Audrey planned the first family outing they'd had in over a decade. They went to the beach, something Audrey, her husband, and their daughters had always talked about doing but never found the time for. She dusted off her grandma's recipe box and started cooking nightly for her family—and twice for me, when I was able to be there in person. I remember sitting in her kitchen, watching her move around with a joy and energy that seemed to defy her prognosis. She was living, really living, and it was beautiful to witness.

Audrey also found a way to meditate that didn't involve

shutting down her ever-ticking brain. She had always wanted to give it a shot, but she stopped when she found no possible way to stop thinking—a common misconception with meditation. I told her there are apps that will guide her through thousands of meditations, and all she had to do was pick the one that worked best for her mood, thoughts, and feelings. I'll never forget her face when I told her other everyday activities like riding a bike, washing the dishes, or even silent car rides could be forms of meditation, too. "Look for those moments that allow you to be present," I told her. She would walk through the forest near her home, forest bathing. This is when someone immerses themselves in the atmosphere of the forest, taking it all in as a way to ease their mind and body. For Audrey, it became a form of therapy. She told me she felt more connected to herself and the world during those walks than she ever had in her whole life.

Then there was the surgery. She survived. I visited Audrey in the hospital and brought her some fake plants to remind her of the walks she'd get back to in the coming months. Her family visited and they played games and even had movie nights when the nice nurses were on duty and let them stay well after visiting hours, quietly. Audrey was determined to heal faster than predicted so she could get back to living, but after five months and a total recovery, the living she so badly wanted to do was no longer a priority. One day, we caught up at a teahouse, and I could see the heaviness in her eyes.

"I don't know what happened," she said, her voice barely

above a whisper. "I got better, and then it was like everything went back to the way it was." Audrey's new job was just like the old one. The family outings stopped. The meditations stopped. The forest walks stopped. Audrey stopped living.

I am glad that I was able to still be there—even a little living is better than none at all. Audrey's story is one I've seen play out many times. When there's no longer the immediate threat of death, life stops being so important. We return to our old habits, old fears, old ways of being. The urgency fades, and we forget the lessons we learned when we thought time was running out. That book we were going to write will get done eventually, the friends we were going to reconcile with can wait, and the life we truly want will be there waiting for us whenever we get to it. I've seen too many people—myself included—lose at this game.

But here's the thing I needed Audrey to know: Living intentionally doesn't have to mean overhauling your entire life every day. It's not about clinging to that same intensity of facing death but rather carrying small pieces of what you learned into your everyday moments. Pausing to actually taste the crème brûlée between sentences, calling your brother to say hi, or writing a single paragraph of that book instead of waiting for the perfect time to sit and write the whole thing. Intentional living is not about perfection; it's about presence. Even a single mindful act each day can keep you connected to the life you wanted when time feels short.

Living and dying are not opposites. They are part of the

same continuum, each informing and enhancing the other. To be a death doula is to be a life doula. It's about helping people live fully, authentically, and unapologetically in these years, months, or just days they have left.

My work is to help people see that now—right now—is the only time they have.

I've sat with many other folks like Silvia and Isaac as they've faced their mortality, and the fear, the regret, and the longing in their eyes is always so familiar. But I've also seen something else. I've seen a spark of courage, just like I saw in Audrey. When that's embraced, even just for a little while, for me, it's like finally seeing that fantastic creature that's only existed in stories. It's magic.

MY FATHER

MY FATHER, FOR ME, REPRESENTS AN ENTIRE GENeration of Black folks who want nothing to do with death—not even their own.

My life as a storyteller, documentary filmmaker, and human has always been about confronting the stories many would rather ignore—those difficult, painful narratives that are hard to hear and harder to see. From the raw truths of sexual assault to the silent struggles of mental health, to the fight for survival under the weight of American tyranny, I have dedicated much of myself to giving these stories a voice. So when it came to death—a topic so often avoided, especially in Black American communities—I knew I had to be just as loud.

Death, for many Black folks, is a subject often left on the table, untouched. There's not even so much as a whisper about it. I've been a conscious witness to this avoidance since I was nine years old, and maybe long before that. After more than three decades, it no longer baffles me, but I would love to see that change.

The silence around death is a cultural, historical, and spiritual phenomenon that stretches across generations. The beautiful thing, however, is that every so often, it'll skip a generation and we'll get folks—like my grandmother, Irene—who are never afraid to talk about death with anyone else who will listen. To do the work of a death doula, it's imperative that I never ignore the deep trauma rooted in American racism or pretend the mistrust of health-care systems isn't warranted. I truly understand that because of these things, among others, death has been viewed as something to avoid discussing, preparing for, or even acknowledging until it taps us on the shoulder, letting us know it's our turn. Sadly, this avoidance has significant consequences for the dying and the families left behind. They must grapple with grief, unanswered questions, and the financial and emotional toll of last-minute end-of-life decisions.

As far back as I can remember, I've watched the generations before me die without any real planning. Even those blessed to have a deathbed didn't want to discuss funeral plans and would say things like "Do whatever you feel is best" to whoever stepped up to handle the business of it all. The only preparation for death for many of those I've worked with, grew up with, and was raised by is a life insurance policy, and even that, in many cases, feels like an afterthought—often with no clear understanding of whether it's even enough to cover funeral expenses. Unfortunately, these days, it often isn't. This is the norm for so many Black families I know. Death is simply not a topic of discussion. The result is a cycle where we are always scrambling, piecing together fragmented stories and memories, left to wonder how our loved ones truly wanted to be given back to the earth and remembered.

My father, like many in his generation, does not want to face the reality of death. Relationships and connections have always been a major part of my development. Given that, I have always paid close attention to how people are connected and relationships are honored. My father had a lot of friends when I was a kid, and I loved being around them, hearing their stories about how Charlottesville used to be, the cabarets, the stunts and pranks they pulled, and the great loves they all claimed to fumble. Now when I ask my father about those men and women, it breaks my heart to learn that so many of them have died. How did I not know this? My ears were always listening for news of death. It didn't take me long to realize my father simply didn't share that information. He moved on with his life after each death as though their lives were never intertwined.

While my father chose to move through life without lingering on loss, others, like Bobby, found themselves unable to escape the weight of grief. Where my father's silence created distance, Bobby's struggle brought him closer to confronting the reality of death head-on.

He called me one day, his voice shaky, the kind of unsteadiness you hear when someone's been holding in more than they should. He said he'd lost another friend and his shoulders weren't strong enough for the weight of grief. Crying alone in the dark had become his ritual, something he'd done after each loss. "It's all I know," he said. His entire life, death had only been spoken about at funerals; once the casket was lowered, the subject was buried, too. But now, sitting in the bathroom, away from his wife, his grandbabies, and the world, tears streaming down his face, he was sinking into a depression he wasn't sure he could handle. He called me because he didn't know how to carry this grief anymore, how to release it in a way that wouldn't swallow him whole. Together we unpacked his pain—piece by piece, death by death—and I helped him find ways to grieve that didn't require being alone in the dark. It wasn't easy for him to trust that process, but he knew that what he'd been doing wasn't working anymore.

William, my dad's friend, was in the hospital dying. This was a man who affectionately called me "Mouse Titty" from the time I was born and over the next forty years. I learned about the cancer from William's niece, and my immediate thought was how I would break the news to my dad. He couldn't have known, I thought. Otherwise, he would have told me.

We were in his kitchen, where we usually talk because he's always cooking, and I asked if he knew William was near death. He knew but didn't want to think too much about it. I kept talking, knowing the pain that comes with the regret of not being there for a friend in the end. I urged him to go. He said he hadn't been yet because he couldn't bring himself to see William in the hospital. Not because he didn't care but because hospitals are triggering for him. They represent death in a way that terrifies him—the place where the final moments unfold, where there's no more denial, no more avoidance. I could see the pain in his eyes, the fear of confronting something so final, so inevitable, that he would rather stay away than say goodbye to his friend.

This experience with my father isn't unique. Many Black Americans, especially older generations, carry the trauma of witnessing death in ways that were often brutal or dehumanizing, from the legacies of slavery and lynching to a healthcare system that has historically failed us. Research highlights these failures starkly. For instance, a 2016 study from the University of Virginia, the very hospital William was dying in and that my father was born in, found that 50 percent of white medical students and residents in the study held false beliefs about biological differences between Black and white individuals, and that those false beliefs were likely to contribute to lower pain ratings of Black clients by their doctors.* The proof is that Black patients have often received less effective pain management compared to white patients. This systemic neglect and bias reinforce a cultural silence around death, dying, and health care, extending beyond personal

* Kelly M. Hoffman, Sophie Trawalter, Jordan R. Axt, and M. Norman Oliver, "Racial Bias in Pain Assessment and Treatment Recommendations, and False Beliefs about Biological Differences between Blacks and Whites," *Proceedings of the National Academy of Sciences of the United States of America* 113, no, 16 (April 2016): 4296–301, https://pmc.ncbi.nlm.nih.gov/articles/PMC4843483/.

avoidance, leading to the mistrust of my father and the many people he represents to me.

The focus in our community has often been on survival rather than preparation for death. We pour our energy into living in a world that wasn't designed for us, navigating systemic racism, economic instability, and a medical system that doesn't always treat us with dignity. In the midst of this, death is relegated to the background, something we'll "deal with when it happens." The problem is, when death does come, we are unprepared. We don't have conversations about wills, advance directives, or funeral plans. We don't ask our loved ones how they want to die or what they want to leave behind. This absence of planning adds layers of stress and grief when death inevitably comes.

And we must not forget about religion when we're discussing why Black Americans are so silent on the topic of death. For many in the Black community, faith is a source of strength, and the church has long been the cornerstone of spiritual and emotional support. But far too often, faith frames death as something to be feared or endured rather than embraced. Congregants are told to have faith in God's plan, but they are rarely encouraged to discuss what that plan might look like when it's time for them to transition. The idea that "God will take care of it" can sometimes prevent us from taking control of our own dying process. As a result, families are left to navigate the aftermath without clear guidance or understanding of their loved ones' wishes.

I remember Margaret, whose deep faith was the central part of her life. Margaret called me because she was anxious and uncertain and didn't want her kids "looking for hay in needlestacks" like she'd done when her mother died unprepared. She tried talking to her pastor, who told her all she needed to do was pray and leave the rest up to God, but that left her in a deeper state of confusion, especially when the doctor started asking about advanced directives and she was alone in the room. The beliefs she was raised with were regretfully passed on to her sons, and they felt discussing death was unnecessary, which only added to Margaret's sense of isolation. I showed up just in time. Together, in private because she didn't want her sons judging her, we made sure her wishes were clearly documented. This process not only gave Margaret a sense of control but also equipped her family with what we hoped would be the understanding they needed to support her in a way that honored her faith and personal wishes. She died just two weeks after we began our journey together, and while I wish she had more time to prepare, I'm glad she finally found peace in the end. No surprise, her sons were also very thankful for everything we were able to put in place with such short notice, and they began conversations with their family about doing the same.

This silence around death must be broken. Conversations about death need to become part of our family dialogues, our community meetings, and even our church sermons. Death is a natural part of life, and by avoiding talking about it, we deny ourselves the opportunity to prepare, to grieve fully, and to honor the lives we've lived.

In my work as a death doula, I've seen firsthand how powerful these conversations can be. By helping families talk openly about death, I've witnessed the peace it brings to both the dying and their loved ones. It's not an easy conversation to have, but it's a necessary one. I've seen families torn apart by confusion and conflict when there was no clear plan in place—children left to argue over funeral arrangements, spouses unsure of how to honor their partner's final wishes. While the people at the end of their life often think it's best to not bring up these difficult conversations while they are alive, in an attempt to avoid stress and any battles, what happens when they die is sometimes a full-blown war that ends when the next person dies. These are situations that can be avoided if we break the silence and start talking about death before it's too late.

For Black Americans, this shift is particularly important. We need to reclaim the narrative around death, to take control of our dying process in ways that honor our history, culture, and spiritual beliefs. This doesn't mean abandoning faith or putting our trust in places that haven't earned it but rather integrating it all with practical planning. It means having conversations about how we want to die, who we want by our side, and how we want to be remembered. It means preparing for death in a way that allows us to live fully, knowing that we've left our loved ones with a clear understanding of our wishes.

Breaking the silence around death is not about planning

for the inevitable—it's about healing generational trauma, reclaiming our right to a dignified death, and ensuring that our final moments reflect the lives we've lived. By speaking openly about death, we create space for love, connection, and peace. For me, that's the most important legacy we can leave behind.

If you're wondering how we can change things for future generations so they don't carry the same fear, silence, and avoidance as my father and his friends are, it starts with having the hard conversations now.

We've all seen it: the way people—especially adults—will sidestep any conversation about death like it's an obstacle they'd rather never face. They'll change the subject, make an awkward joke, or walk away altogether. I've seen it in my father's eyes, in the tightness of his jaw when the subject of someone's death comes up. I've heard it in Bobby's voice when, after years of avoiding it, he finally broke down and admitted that the deaths of friends had quietly eaten away at him for years. This silence, this avoidance—it's passed down generation after generation, as if not talking about death will keep it from ever happening.

But here's the thing: Death is coming for all of us, and silence has never been strong enough to keep it away. Silence makes things worse. I know this because I've worked with families who were completely unprepared to deal with the death of a loved one—not because they didn't care but because they didn't know where to begin. And the root of that is simple: We've made death an unbearable topic. We treat it like something dark and unspeakable, as if daring to talk about it might somehow invite it into our lives.

Younger generations are picking up on this avoidance, and they're growing up just like the adults I meet all too often—people who absolutely refuse to have a conversation about their own death or the death of someone they love. It's time to break that cycle. We can't keep passing this fear down like an heirloom. If we want things to be different for the next generation, we have to start now, making conversations around death not just easier to bear but a natural part of life.

So, what do we do? How do we change the conversation so that younger generations don't carry the same fear and avoidance into their adulthood? I believe it starts with how we talk about death early on. Instead of whispering about it behind closed doors, or waiting until it's too late to have the conversation, we can normalize it. We can make it a part of life, something to plan for and discuss openly.

For parents, this means being honest with their kids. When a pet, friend, or grandparent dies, that's an opportunity to have real conversations about what it means to die, what happens after, and how we can prepare for it. Avoiding the topic with children, thinking that we're protecting them, only makes it harder for them later on. They grow up with the same discomfort and fear that we've carried, and then when it's time to face death in their own lives, they'll be just as unprepared as we were. In the words of Frederick Douglass, "It is easier to build strong children than to repair broken men."

We don't have to make death a heavy, depressing subject. We can bring light into the conversation. That's the gift we can give to the next generation—the peace of knowing that death is not some looming monster to be feared but a part of the journey we're all on. When we talk about it openly, we take away its power. It becomes something we can face together, instead of something we hide from.

The key is starting small, having the conversations in ways that feel natural. We can talk about what we want when we die—how we want to be remembered, what kind of send-off we'd like, who we want to make decisions for us if we're not able to make them ourselves. These are conversations we should be having not just when death is near but all the time. Imagine how much easier it would be if the kids in our lives grew up hearing these conversations, knowing it's okay to talk about death, to ask questions, to express their fears. They wouldn't have to carry the same burdens that we did.

And let's be real, this isn't just for them. This is for us, too. Talking about death doesn't just prepare the people we'll leave behind; it gives us peace, too. It's liberating to know that we've thought about it, that we've made plans. There's a freedom in acknowledging that death is a part of life, and in doing so, we give ourselves permission to live more fully.

We don't need to wait for the perfect moment or the "right time." There's never a perfect time. Start now. Bring it up at dinner. Make it part of your family's narrative.

I've seen too many adults grow up avoiding death until it's

standing right in front of them. I've seen the pain it causes—the way it steals from them, not just in their final moments but in the days, months, and years leading up to it. We can stop that. We can teach that death is not something to fear but something to face with grace, love, and clarity.

It starts with us, right now.

COLSTON

ONE AFTERNOON, WHILE I WAS REWORKING A RECipe in an attempt to get as close to the ramen I had in a little Tokyo alley shop, with the window open letting the neighbors smell what was happening in my cabin, my phone buzzed. It was a physician friend who provides medical aid in dying. His voice was steady but carried a worry I recognized immediately. He asked if I could be a death doula for his patient, Colston, a man whose journey, I would soon learn, was as complex as the choice he'd made. Colston, facing a rapid decline due to an advanced brain tumor, requested medical aid but was alone, with no family or friends to support his decision. His physician, my friend, knew the importance of having someone present to offer emotional and practical support during such a critical time, and with Colston's permission, he reached out to me.

I couldn't help but think back to the first time I learned about medical aid in dying. I was a teenager, and Dr. Jack Kevorkian was at the center of controversy for assisting terminally ill patients who wanted to end their lives. Even being that young, I remember thinking, "If people want to leave, they should have every right, and people should be allowed to be there to help them however they can." Of course, at that time, Kevorkian's work was seen by many as immoral, even illegal, and of course it was heavily criticized. But what Kevorkian began—what seemed radical back then—has evolved today into a more accepted, albeit still complex, conversation about the rights of those facing terminal illness. The work he pioneered, though controversial, laid the foundation for what we now call medical aid in dying, a practice that's becoming more normalized in parts of the world, giving people the option to make their own decision about when and how they go.

When I received the call, my immediate questions were: What is Colston's current physical and emotional state? What is the timeline for the process? Are there any legal requirements I should be aware of? How can I best support you as the physician? What should I expect when the medicine is taken? I had a ton of questions about Colston I kept myself from asking, deciding it'd be better to ask Colston face to face. I was also filled with a mix of emotions. This was uncharted territory for me. My respect for those who choose medical aid in dying was then and is now unwavering, yet I wondered about Colston's inner thoughts and feelings. Would he be certain of his decision? Would he need reassurance? Would I be present when he changed his mind and it was too late? My initial uncertainty was soon eased by the profound clarity I sensed in Colston when we finally met, the two of us in his doorway, hugging like we'd known each other for decades.

I was greeted by a man whose strength and resolve were palpable. Despite his declining health, Colston was determined to not only be a gracious host, offering me the grapefruit juice and turkey bacon he had ready, knowing how much I loved them both, but he was also determined to make the most of his final days. We slowly toured both floors of his home, and as I looked at all the wonderful things he had collected, hung up, spread across tables, and saved for others to experience, I was able to piece together what must have been an incredibly beautiful and rewarding life. As he talked about the items I took special interest in, I was reminded of one of the reasons I do this work: It gives me the opportunity to see just how fantastic life can be. The statue made of stone he'd bought in a Moroccan souk from a man who refused to bargain. The wooden box that held letters, postcards, wedding invitations, and notes written on scrap paper was made for him in a Chinese fishing village by a man who made even better tea. The fabric that wrapped the box was made by a woman in a small town in northern Ghana who let him add a few stitches before she completed it. We spent the first three days in conversations about all of his travels and what he hoped for in the coming days.

Colston wanted to leave behind personal messages for his nieces and nephews, so we spent hours at his dining room table writing letters to each of them. He talked as I wrote, giving me permission to edit any part of what he said, but I assured him his words were as clear as anything I could possibly add or change them into. Each letter was deeply personal—not just a farewell to the children he often considered his own but a hopeful map they could follow should they ever need to find a way. "I want them to live boldly and freely like I did," Colston said.

We also worked on recording his obituary. Colston had a poignant request regarding this task: "Something about it being on paper right now seems strange," he said. I promised him I would honor his wishes and write it out after his death.

Colston's family, though unwilling to be present during his final moments, showed up regularly to "get on his last nerves" and love on him immensely. They brought him his favorite foods—key lime pie, liver and onions, cornbread. Colston barely ate any of it, but he insisted I enjoy the meals. I did, and they were delicious reminders of the comfort found in shared traditions and familiar tastes. I told Colston about the big bowls of potato salad I watched my grandma make in her living room, to be carried to the sick and shut-in folks who were deeply loved by my grandma or by the people ordering the big bowl of love.

"It's what we do," he said. We take care of each other. I asked how he felt about his family not wanting to be there when the time came to die, and he forced a smile and easily said, "This isn't something everyone can handle. It's okay."

To those of you with family or friends nearing the end of

their lives and questioning whether to be there when the time comes, I want to encourage you to show up, if you can. Being there isn't just for them; it's for you, too. There's something powerful about sitting with someone in their final moments, a way to honor their life by walking with them as far as you can. It's an intimate, sacred experience that, hard as it may be, offers peace and connection that lingers long after they're gone. The first time I was with someone near the end, I was twelve. My cousin Maine came home to die, and I didn't fully grasp what it meant for him and me. But looking back, I'm grateful to know he wasn't alone. Being there for him, even at that young age, shaped how I understand the importance of presence.

The morning Colston had chosen to end his life came quickly, and I awoke with a sense of unease. My thoughts were filled with apprehension that perhaps Colston might suddenly be unsure of what to do when the decision needed to be made in just a couple of hours. When I entered the living room, there was Colston, dressed in attire imbued with personal significance. He wore pants from a trip to Tanzania, a gift from a past lover who loved the way he looked in them. His shirt was from his sister. She'd stopped by earlier that morning to kiss and hug her brother goodbye and give him the shirt she knew he'd look his best in. On his head was his father's hat. He told me his father wore that hat every day, and when he died, Colston's mother made sure it went to him. The blanket beside him, knitted by his mother, added a final touch of familial warmth.

Colston radiated a serene joy as he prepared for this monumental moment. I've seen this look many times with clients who knew death was near and they were running toward it like a kid toward summer. I sat beside him and asked if he felt ready. Without hesitation, he took my hand and affirmed that he was as ready as he had ever been about anything. His only concern was whether the doctor would arrive with the medication as planned.

The doctor arrived. Colston made us a pot of rooibos and shared his dream with us. He dreamed the doctor called and said his death would need to be postponed for reasons unknown. He replied to Colston that many patients share a common fear—that when the time comes, the doctor won't show up, and they'll be forced to postpone the moment they've been mentally and emotionally preparing for. This fear can manifest in dreams where the date is delayed, the medication is unavailable, or circumstances beyond their control keep them from ending their suffering when they're ready. They often wake up panicked, believing the dream is real, gripped by the anxiety of losing control over one of the few things they feel they still have power over: the timing of their own death. For many, the ability to choose is a source of comfort, and the thought of that choice being taken away, even temporarily, can be overwhelming.

Before taking the medication, Colston shared a confession. Initially he had wanted to die alone but had reconsidered for two reasons. The first was that he wanted someone he shared his life with to hold his hand as he slipped away, and he thanked me for allowing him to share pieces of his life over the last few days. Second, he needed someone there to read a poem he loved. He walked to his bookshelf where we'd placed the letters to his nieces and nephews and grabbed a folded piece of lined notebook paper. He handed me a folded piece of paper with a poem written in ink. Colston asked me to wait a few moments after he took the medication before reading it aloud. "You'll know when." It was a deeply personal request, and I promised to honor it.

Colston administered the medication himself, then settled onto his sofa, pulling his mother's blanket over him and placing his father's hat on his chest. The doctor and I watched the hat move up and down in rhythm and we looked at one another, with no words exchanged. Colston's face was calm, and peace was present. Then he smiled. I knew that was my signal.

Colston once told me that Audre Lorde's words made him feel, as she says in the poem, "named in a world that didn't always want to see me." That poem had been a companion during years of isolation and reckoning. And now, as his body began to drift toward death, it was the anchor he reached for.

I began reading, and even though his eyes were closed, I could tell he was still listening. The lines weren't long—but they held weight. The poem speaks to those "who live at the shoreline," those who know what it is to exist in uncertainty, at the edge of something vast and final. That had always been

Colston—balancing between what the world demanded of him and what he could offer in return.

I spoke the line about how "we are afraid our words will not be heard," and I thought of all the ways Colston had tried to be understood in his life—through art, through protest, through silence. And still, he kept speaking. Kept showing up.

In the final lines, I read just enough for him to hear what he already knew in his bones: that "we were never meant to survive" was not a sentence of despair, but a declaration of truth—and of resistance.

I finished reading, and didn't say anything more. The poem had already said it all.

The doctor and I waited in silence, our breathing nearly in sync with Colston's until his breathing stopped.

His family arrived hours later, paying their respects and offering support to each other. His sister pulled me aside, crying, wishing she'd made a different decision and stayed with me and Colston. Despite their initial absence, their love and care were evident in the way they honored Colston's memory.

Colston's choice to seek medical aid in dying was not a decision made lightly. It was a choice that allowed him to maintain control in a situation where control had been stripped away by illness. For many, the option provides not only an end but a sense of relief and agency. Even if individuals do not ultimately follow through, having this option often brings a measure of peace and a sense of control over the dying process.

To those of you considering medical aid in dying, I want to start by saying that whatever you decide, it's your decision, and it's the right one for you. As a death doula, my role is not to steer you in one direction or another but to support you in whatever decision you make. After walking this road with Colston, I've come to see that this choice—choosing medical aid in dying—is about dignity. It's about deciding for yourself how you want your story to end. There's a peace that comes with knowing you have a say in your final chapter, even when everything else feels out of control.

If you're considering this option, my advice is to be sure of your reasons and to make space for your emotions along the way. Talk to your loved ones, if you can, and let them know how you're feeling, but know that ultimately this is about what's right for you. Surround yourself with people who will support you, whether it's a doctor, a friend, or someone like me, a death doula, who can help you navigate the emotional complexities of this process. If you have any questions, ask them. If you have any fears, share them. Know that you don't have to carry this alone and that making this decision is an act of incredible courage.

If someone you love has made this choice, it's okay to feel confused, sad, or even angry. You might not understand their reasons, and that's okay. Showing up for them with an open heart is what's important—listen without judgment; ask questions to understand, not to convince. This decision is deeply personal, and while it may be hard to accept, your presence and support can offer them more comfort than you realize. Sometimes just being there is enough. Give yourself permission to sit with those emotions without rushing to resolve them. It's okay to not have all the answers right away. Take the time you need to process, and remember that understanding can unfold slowly, especially when it comes to something as complex as this.

The world is starting to catch up to what many of us have known for a long time: Death with dignity is a right.

If you're reading this and wondering if you have what it takes to do this work, let me tell you right now: You absolutely do. My first time supporting someone through medical aid in dying was with Colston, and I had so many questions about what I was stepping into. I wondered if I could provide the emotional strength and comfort he needed. But when I met him, I was quickly reminded that being a death doula is about being there, sitting in the uncomfortable space with someone, and letting them know they're not alone. And in that, I found the strength to provide as much comfort as Colston needed.

You already have what it takes. You don't have to be an expert on death. You just need to be present and trust that your compassion is enough. In the hardest moments, when you feel like you're not sure what to do, just remember: Being there is the most important thing you can offer. And that is more than enough.

DYING WITH FEWER REGRETS IN EIGHT STEPS

BY NOW YOU KNOW I LOVE TALKING ABOUT DEATH and the importance of living the life we want to help us get the death we want. Because of my passion for this topic and how often I share it, not only here but every place I go, I'm often asked by those brave enough to stand around and listen to me, "What do I do so I don't get to the end regretting everything?" Or some version of that.

It's a big question and not an easy one to answer. Honestly, sometimes I'm just as caught up in it as they are. I do know one thing: Living a life we want that leads to a death with fewer regrets is about making peace with who you are, what you want, and who you want to become. It's about being intentional. Yeah, I know you've heard that a million times before, but it's true. The many friends and wise folks in your family who've told you this same thing are right. As a death doula and a curious writer who's attempting to get the world to open up and share the parts of them that happen between birth and death, I often ask my clients the hard questions. As you read and work through these, know these are the ones that resonated best with the folks I've worked with.

Step 1: Get Honest with Yourself

The first step in dying with fewer regrets is get honest with yourself. What are you afraid of? What do you avoid because it's uncomfortable? What have you been running from, numbing out to, or ignoring because it feels too big or too heavy? I promise you, whatever you avoid in life will come creeping in when you're facing death. Trust me, I've seen it time and time again. So, we might as well unpack it now while we still have time to make different choices.

Ask yourself:

1. What am I afraid to admit about my life, my relationships, or myself?
2. What stories am I telling myself that no longer serve me?
3. If I knew I had six months to live, what would suddenly seem important, and what would lose its grip on me?

These questions force you to look at what's holding you back. The fears, the lies, the stories we tell ourselves—they all keep us stuck in lives that don't feel truly lived. But when you shine a light on them, when you see them for what they are, you can start making choices that are in sync with your truth, not your fear.

Step 2: Embrace Your Mortality

Embracing your mortality might sound terrifying—I know, death is the big, scary thing we all want to avoid. But what if embracing your mortality is actually the thing that sets you free to live? What if understanding that your time is limited makes every moment richer, more sacred?

I want you to sit with the thought of your death. Not in a morbid way—unless you really want to—but in a way that says, "Okay, I know this is coming. What does it mean for how I want to live?" Because here's the deal: The death of your friends, your parents, your grandma, and just about everyone except you should be a constant reminder to you that time is winding up. If you want to die with fewer regrets, live like the clock is ticking. Don't put off what's important to you. Don't wait until you have more money, more time, or more confidence. Inspired by *The Usual Suspects*: The greatest trick life ever played was convincing us we have more time than we do.

Ask yourself:

1. If I truly embraced that my time is limited, what would I change about my life?
2. What relationships would I heal, deepen, or let go of?
3. What risks have I been avoiding because I thought I had time to figure it out later?

With these questions, I invite you to stop living as if you have unlimited tomorrows. Tomorrow may not come, and you're wasting time on things that don't bring you joy—on things that don't serve you. Stop waiting. Take whatever action needs to be taken now.

Step 3: Finding Your Truth

Many of us are out here living lives that don't belong to us. We're doing what's expected, what's comfortable, or what pleases someone else. But to live in a way that leads to fewer regrets, you've got to figure out your truth and live it unapologetically. But it has to be your truth—not what society tells you to want, not what your parents wanted for you, and not what you think you should be doing for others.

So, what does that mean in practice? It means you've got to slow down and ask yourself what you want out of this one life. What lights you up? What pulls you in? What's that thing you've been wanting to do but haven't allowed yourself to fully dream about?

Here's a little secret that isn't truly a secret because we all know it, even if it's buried really deep: People tend to regret the things they didn't do more than the things they did. The dreams they didn't chase. The risks they didn't take. The person they didn't reconnect with or even ask out. The passions they didn't follow because life got in the way.

Ask yourself:

1. What is true for me? What do I know in my bones that I've been ignoring or pushing aside?
2. What dreams have I been too afraid to chase? What's holding me back from pursuing them?
3. Who do I want to become, and what steps do I need to take to start becoming that person today?

Let's confront the parts of your life that aren't aligned with your truth. These questions push you to face the dreams you've been too scared to pursue and to make choices that reflect the person you want to become, not the person you think you *should* be.

Step 4: Telling Your Story

Your stories matter—not just in death, but in how you choose to live every day. I talk a lot about dying with stories, but I want you to live with your stories, too. It's not enough to live passively. You need to live in a way that you're consciously creating moments, memories, and experiences that become part of your narrative. When I sit with someone at the end of their life, we talk about their stories—the moments that mattered, the ones that shaped them. Please don't mistake me here: These stories aren't always big grand gestures. Sometimes they're small, quiet moments that made life feel full. Hector reflected on the time he did mushrooms in a jungle in Belize with a shaman and a sex worker. Teddy remembered playing Clue at the kitchen table with his wife on Fridays after putting the kids to bed. Those moments mattered.

When I'm teaching others to unlock and unblock the writer within, I remind them that their life is indeed a story, and they are the author. I ask, "Are you writing a story you're proud of? Are you living in a way that feels true to who you are? If not, there is still time to change the narrative." When I want to put some fire under them, I add, "But we don't know how much time that is." To you, I say it's time to step into the role of active participant, not just a bystander. Don't let life happen to you. Grab the pen and start writing it.

Ask yourself:

1. What are the stories I want to tell now? What are the stories I want to tell when it's my time to go?
2. What moments do I want to create now that will become part of my legacy?
3. If my life were a book that was published today, would I be proud of the story? If not, what needs to change?

It's time you start living as the main character of your own life. These questions prompt you to think about the moments you're creating now and the legacy you want to leave. Are you proud of the life you're living? If not, these questions guide you to start rewriting your story while there's still time.

Step 5: Letting Go of Perfection

The idea that we must get everything perfect is one of the biggest blocks to living the life we truly want. We think, "I can't start that family until I have everything figured out," or "I can't travel the world until I have enough money." The truth is, there's never going to be a perfect time. Life is messy, and if you're waiting for perfection, you're going to be waiting for a long time.

So, let go of the idea that everything must be lined up before you can start living the way you want. You don't need the perfect conditions. You just need to start. You need to be willing to take imperfect action. The stories you'll want to tell at the end aren't going to be about how perfectly you executed every plan—they'll be about how you showed up in the messiness of life and embraced it anyway.

Ask yourself:

1. Where am I holding back because I think I'm not ready or it's not the right time?
2. What would it look like to take imperfect action toward the life I want?
3. How can I give myself permission to embrace the messiness of life and let go of the need to have it all figured out?

Why are you waiting for "perfect" when you can start living *now*? These questions push you to act even if it's messy, even if you don't have all the answers. Make that permission slip now.

Step 6: Connecting with Others

True connection is what life comes down to, especially when everything else falls away. When I sit with people at the end of their life, they rarely talk about their job, their money, or the things they accumulated. They talk about love. They talk about the people who mattered to them and the relationships that shaped their life. The way you connect with others—how you love, how you show up, how you give and receive—is a huge part of living a life with fewer regrets.

Ask yourself:

1. Who are the people who matter most to me, and how am I showing up for them?
2. Am I giving and receiving love fully, or am I holding back out of fear, pride, or past hurt?
3. What relationships do I need to mend, nurture, or let go of to live in alignment with the person I want to be?

These questions help you focus on the people in your life who push you to look at how you're showing up for those who matter most and how you're allowing love into your life. We don't always pay attention to the connections in our lives even though they are often a large part of what defines us.

Step 7: Defining Your Own Success

We often fall into the trap of believing that success has a single, universal definition—one tied to money, power, and fame. But shouldn't real success be living a life that's aligned with what you value most? It's about knowing what makes you feel alive, what makes your heart beat loudly, and living in a way that honors that.

You have to define success for yourself. Otherwise you'll spend your life chasing someone else's version of it, only to reach the end and realize it never mattered to you.

Ask yourself:

1. What does success look like for me? Not what I've been told, not what society expects, but what really matters to me?
2. Am I living in alignment with my definition of success, or am I chasing something that doesn't truly fulfill me?
3. What small shifts can I make today to live in a way that feels like true success to me?

These questions help you stop chasing someone else's dream and start living for what truly matters to you. They force you to define success on your own terms and make choices that reflect that, so you don't reach the end of your life realizing you were chasing something that never mattered to you.

Step 8: Reflecting, Adjusting, and Living with Intention

A life with fewer regrets almost always begins with regular reflection, thoughtful adjustments, and the courage to live with intention. You're going to grow. You're going to change. What mattered to you at twenty-five might not matter at fifty. And that's okay. The key is to keep checking in with yourself and making sure you're still living in alignment with who you are and what you want.

Ask yourself:

1. Am I living in alignment with my values, my truth, and my definition of success right now?
2. What adjustments do I need to make to live more fully and intentionally?
3. How can I make reflection and self-awareness a regular part of my life so that I'm always steering myself toward the life I want to live?

These questions help you stay on track. They remind you that life is fluid, and what matters most can shift as you grow and change. By regularly and critically reflecting on where you are and where you want to be, you can make sure you're always moving toward the life that feels true to you.

Start today. Ask yourself these questions. Get honest, get messy, and most importantly, live. Because at the end of the day, that's what it's all about—living fully, loving deeply, and leaving this world with as few regrets as possible.

SPEAKING ILL OF THE DEAD

JIANNA WAS ON THE VERGE OF LOSING HER FATHER, who was in hospice care, and she didn't know how to show up for him in his final days. Normally this would be a familiar situation, people wrestling with how to say goodbye, how to be present, how to find closure. The week before, I'd helped a man find ways to be there for his father at the end of his life. That call was easy because his father was easy and loving and supported his son in creating an incredible life. I told him to be present physically and emotionally and to let his father know just how much he meant to him and to the world. I told him to share his gratitude and the memories he held near and dear. In those moments, it's never about being perfect or saying the proper things but about holding the space, holding hands, and allowing silence to speak as much as the words. But this was different. The thing was, her father had been, in her words, "the shittiest dad," and by most accounts, not a great person either.

When Jianna called, I could hear the conflict in her voice. It wasn't just the sadness of impending loss; it was something much deeper, grittier, and rawer. The words she spoke were mixed with intense emotions—anger, resentment, guilt, confusion. How was she supposed to act like a loving daughter when all he'd ever been was hurtful and neglectful? How do you sit by someone's deathbed when part of you has been waiting for this moment so you can be free?

As we talked, I shared a quote from Anne Lamott that I keep tucked away to share with anyone who'll listen, especially those ready to write and speak their truths. "You own everything that happened to you. Tell your stories. If people wanted you to write warmly about them, they should have behaved better." It's a simple but powerful truth. Your experience is your own, and no one—not even death—can take that from you.

Jianna talked about the times her father said he'd show up, but didn't. She talked about the summers her mom would force her to spend with him and how he had her sleeping on couches in his friends' homes, feeling unsafe, because he refused to work and refused to properly provide for her. There were never words of encouragement or stories told at her bedside, and gifts were rare, if ever. She remembered the way he'd belittle her, dismissing her dreams and needs as if they were inconveniences.

"I was a burden, not a daughter," Jianna said. His own desires were far above his responsibilities as a father.

I remembered and shared with Jianna a story I'd heard

many years back about a woman on her deathbed asking to see the daughter she'd treated so poorly throughout her entire life. The daughter, time after time, refused to show up, but it never stopped the dying mother from asking. With just a few days left and enough strength for one final plea, she asked the caregiver to reach out to her daughter, letting her know she had only days left. To her surprise, her daughter showed up. She was there only fifteen minutes and used the entire time to tell her mother how horrible she was as a parent and hoped she could forgive herself because it wouldn't come from her. When she was done, her daughter walked out without waiting for a response. The caregiver, who'd sat there the entire time, listening, was shocked, unsure of what to say to the woman lying on the bed, in tears. She simply offered, "I'm sorry she said those things to you."

The mother shook her head and said, "No, that's why I wanted her here. I wanted her to get these things out once and for all." That night, the mother died.

After that story, I told Jianna that it was okay to be honest with him, even in these final days. It was okay to feel conflicted and to not sugarcoat the past just because he was dying. I reminded her that death and dying don't turn a villain into a saint. You have the right to speak your truth, even when that truth is uncomfortable. Honoring your experience means telling the whole story, not just the parts that are easy to remember.

She listened quietly, and I could tell she was taking it all in, trying to process what that would look like—how she could be truthful without being cruel, how she could honor her own experience without feeling like she was betraying some unspoken rule about how we're supposed to treat the dying or the dead.

Truth is, most of us have been taught from a young age that it's wrong to speak ill of the dead or the dying. We're taught they deserve respect at the end of what is often a hard life. I heard it from my grandmothers, aunts, friends with old spirits, and even a few college professors. It's as if once someone dies or reaches the last moment of their existence, all their sins are supposed to be washed away, leaving only the good memories behind. But life, like most things, isn't that neat. People are complicated. They're a mix of good and bad, of kindness and cruelty. Just because someone dies, it doesn't mean that all the hurt they caused disappears. I've walked alongside many who live with a pain they don't know what to do with because it was caused by someone who they can no longer talk to about it.

There are reasons why people are scared to be honest about those who are at the end of life and the dead. For one, there's this idea that it's disrespectful, that we owe them some kind of reverence simply because they've made it to the end or passed on. We don't, especially when their presence brought trauma, strife, grief, and anxiety. There's also the fear of judgment—from others but also from ourselves. Are we bad people if we don't forgive everything? If we can't find it in our hearts to forget the pain they caused?

Called by his son in hopes of softening him up, I once worked with Bert, a dying man who had spent a lifetime causing chaos in the lives of those around him—often purposely. His actions left deep scars on his family, and as he lay on his deathbed, they were convinced his painful end was karma finally catching up with him. Yet he refused to apologize for any of it. In his mind, death would wash away his sins, just as it had for his father, he thought. He believed that once he was gone, all would be forgiven, the slate wiped clean, and the memories of his misdeeds softened by the passing of time. I was unsure of how he was able to hold so tight to that belief, especially after watching the side effects of his father's torment on him manifest daily. But even in those final moments, the hurt Bert had caused remained sharp and unforgiving in the minds of those he left behind, a reminder that death doesn't automatically grant redemption.

I know it's necessary to speak our truth, especially when it comes to someone who had a significant impact on our lives. We can't just sweep things under the rug and pretend they didn't happen. Those collected wrongdoings will catch fire. The sweeping and the hiding and the pretending will lead to more pain down the road—unresolved feelings, unhealed wounds. And honestly, it's a disservice to ourselves to pretend that our experiences don't matter.

Jianna decided to sit with her father and be honest. She'd attempted to do that many times over the years, but for the first time, he wouldn't be able to run, hide, hang up, or talk over her. "You don't have to be brutal to be honest," I told her. She didn't rehash every terrible thing he'd done, but she didn't pretend everything was fine either. Jianna told her father the truth. She didn't get a perfect resolution—life rarely gives us those—but she found some peace in speaking her truth, in not letting the unspoken words fester inside her.

Death doesn't erase the past, but it does give us a chance to confront it. It's not about being cruel or unforgiving; it's about being real. It's about recognizing that our stories matter, that our experiences shape who we are, and that those experiences don't just vanish when someone dies.

You don't have to rewrite history just because someone has passed on. You don't have to pretend that everything was okay if it wasn't. It's okay to feel what you feel, to speak your truth, and to remember that at the end of the day, you own your story.

In a recent conversation with my friend Van, we dived into a topic that hangs in the air for so many family caregivers: the complex emotions that often accompany the death of someone who didn't treat them well. Van brought up this idea with a mix of curiosity and disbelief, wondering how it can feel like a weight has been lifted, even when that weight comes from years of hurt and disappointment.

"It's so common," she said, shaking her head, "and yet so taboo to talk about."

She was right. There's a strange relief that can wash over you, even when the person who's passed was more a source of pain than love. It's as if you've been carrying around an emotional boulder and now it's finally rolling away.

As we chatted, we reflected on how this relief can be quickly tainted by guilt, that nagging voice whispering that you shouldn't feel this way. It's a trap many people fall into, believing that to be relieved is to dishonor the deceased. But I told Van that this feeling, however complicated, is entirely valid. It's not about casting judgment on the life that was lived; it's about acknowledging the reality of your own experience. I shared how important it is to give ourselves permission to feel relief while also grappling with the guilt that follows. Those two emotions can coexist; they are part of healing.

"It's like you have to process both sides," I said. Van nodded, and I could see the gears turning in her mind.

"Acknowledging the pain doesn't erase the good in you," she mused. We agreed that working through these feelings requires bravery. It's an emotional landscape that demands honesty—an honest acknowledgment of what was and what could have been.

I reminded her that allowing ourselves to feel a mix of emotions is not just okay, it's essential. By facing those complex feelings head-on, we can begin to untangle the knot of guilt, resentment, and relief. The truth is, healing doesn't come from ignoring our feelings. It comes from embracing them, understanding them, and ultimately allowing them to guide us to a healthier space. That's how we can move forward—not by rewriting the narrative of our past but by owning every part of our story, even the painful chapters.

Now let's talk about how you can show up for someone who hurt you, especially when they're nearing the end of their life. It's a question that many wrestle with, one that can't be answered lightly because it's layered with emotions—pain, resentment, confusion, and maybe even love buried under years of hurt. Here's what I want you to know: There's no one right answer, but there is your truth, and you're allowed to honor it.

If you decide to show up, remember this: It's not about erasing the past. Showing up doesn't mean you have to pretend everything is okay or that you've miraculously healed from the wounds they caused. You don't have to play the part of the "forgiving saint" just because they're dying. Instead, you can approach it as an opportunity for closure on your terms. It might mean having an honest conversation, like Jianna did, where you acknowledge the hurt without being cruel. It might mean just sitting there in silence, holding their hand, or simply being present in their final moments. That presence can sometimes be as much for you as it is for them.

If you choose to show up, I encourage you to let go of the pressure to fix everything or to find perfect words. Sometimes, being there in whatever capacity you can manage is enough. You don't owe them an apology, a confession, or an erasure of the wrongs they've done. What you owe, if anything, is to yourself—to ensure that you walk away without additional regret, that you've said and done what you feel comfortable with.

And if you decide not to show up, that's okay, too. You don't owe anyone your presence, especially someone who brought you harm. Choosing not to be there doesn't make you a bad person, nor does it mean you're unforgiving or cold. Sometimes the most loving thing you can do for yourself is to protect your peace, and that might look like keeping your distance, especially if being near them would only reopen old wounds.

It's important to remember that showing up can take many forms. Maybe it's writing a letter you never send, or having a conversation with a trusted friend or therapist about your feelings. Maybe your presence is felt in a different way—by choosing to heal yourself and move forward in life with those wounds acknowledged but not continually reopened.

Whatever choice you make, make it with intention. If you show up, let it be because you choose to, not because you feel obligated by some external pressure to do what's expected. If you don't, stand firm in your decision, knowing that taking care of yourself is just as important as anything else.

There is no shame in how you choose to navigate this, whether you walk away or sit by their side. Both paths are valid, and only you can know which one feels truest to you.

THE DEATH RALLY

WHEN RASHAD CALLED ME, I KNEW THIS WAS GOing to be a little harder than most. His voice was filled with a desperation I could feel through the phone, each word trembling with the fear of losing the man he had loved for decades. I was being called to help Miles in his transition, but I also understood that my role was just as much about helping Rashad navigate the emotional labyrinth that lay ahead. Miles, a free spirit and a deeply spiritual artist, had long accepted his mortality, speaking about his impending death with the kind of calm reverence that one might reserve for a sunset or a lover's smile. Rashad, however, couldn't fathom a world without him. That's where I came in.

When I arrived at their home, the air felt thick with the unspoken. The house was a shrine to their love: art covering every wall, evidence of their shared life, framed memories that seemed to hold up the walls. But that vibrancy seemed to shrink as I made my way down the hall to where Miles lay. His body, now a frail version of the man Rashad had fallen in love with, was quiet, resting under the morphine's merciful spell.

I stepped into the room, knowing I had to act quickly. Time is always a slippery thing in situations like this. We only had brief moments of lucidity, brief windows where Miles could communicate before the medication pulled him back under. Rashad hovered near the bed, holding Miles's hand as if it were the last rope tethering him to this world. And in some ways, it was.

"Hey, Miles," I said softly, taking his other hand in mine. His eyes fluttered open, and he gave me a small smile. Rashad's gaze darted between us, fear and hope warring in his eyes. I knew he was grasping for something tangible to hold on to, some way to make sense of everything that was happening. We had spoken on the phone several times before my arrival, and he had confided in me that he didn't know what questions to ask; he didn't know what he needed to hear from me to make peace with what was coming. He was afraid of saying the wrong thing to Miles, to himself, and to me. He was more afraid of wasting what little time they had left.

I decided to start with the questions Rashad was too afraid to voice. "Are you afraid to die, Miles?" I asked gently. Rashad's grip tightened around Miles's hand as if bracing himself for the answer.

Miles looked at me, then at Rashad, and shook his head. "No. I'm not afraid. I just don't want anything to go backward. All the work. I don't want it to be lost," he said. Miles's rolling eyes beneath his heavy eyelids turned upward to Rashad. "And I was enough for you."

Rashad needed to hear those words. Tears welled up in his eyes, and he leaned down to kiss Miles's hand. "You are."

We continued like this, each question pulling back another layer, opening more space for honesty and love.

"Did you do everything you wanted to do?" I asked, watching Miles's face closely.

"There's always more to do, but I did enough," he whispered.

Rashad's tears were flowing freely now, and I told him to let them come. "Let your body do what it needs to do, too," I said. Grief is as much a physical process as it is an emotional one. It must move through us, or it gets stuck.

When Miles needed to rest, Rashad and I would leave the room, retreating to the kitchen where we'd talk about their life together—from their first date to this deathbed. Rashad told me about their first date, how he knew from that night that Miles was it for him. He spoke about the trips they took, the art they made, the fights they had—all of it stamped into their shared existence. And through it all, there was this undercurrent of disbelief, like he still couldn't quite accept that this was happening.

He confessed that he had been researching alternative healing methods, hoping for a miracle. I listened, understanding his need to cling to hope, even if I knew that what he was searching for wouldn't come. It's a delicate balance, holding space for someone's hope while also preparing them for the reality that's unfolding. To do this, we must honor their need to believe in possibilities, no matter how slim, without dismissing the inevitable. This means acknowledging their hopes with compassion while gently guiding them to consider practical matters and emotional preparations. It's about being present, offering comfort without false assurances, and creating an environment where they can express their fears and wishes freely, knowing they're supported regardless of the outcome. Balancing hope and reality require deep empathy, honest communication, and a willingness to sit with uncertainty and pain.

By day three, something shifted. Rashad found his footing, found his voice. He started asking the questions himself, each one a little deeper, a little more honest. "What do you wish we had done together?" he asked one afternoon, his voice steady despite the tears in his eyes.

Miles smiled. "More dancing. More travel. Kids that look like you."

I watched as Rashad absorbed the answer, his body leaning closer to Miles as if he could memorize the feel of him, the sound of his voice, the shape of his words. It was beautiful and heartbreaking, watching them find their way through this together.

Rashad had been carrying a heavy burden of guilt, convinced that if he'd tried harder, he could have prevented Miles's decline. He confided in me one night, tears streaming down his face, that he felt like he had failed his partner. He had clung to the belief that there was something more he could do to fix things. On that third night, when he finally told

Miles how guilty he felt for not being able to save him, Miles scrunched up his face and playfully pretended to slap Rashad across the cheek. I still believe if he was strong enough, that slap would have been real. Rashad laughed through his tears, knowing exactly what Miles was trying to say—that he'd done everything he possibly could. Cancer doesn't relent because of love or effort. Miles knew that, and he needed Rashad to know it, too.

On the fourth night, Rashad and I promised we'd try to get some sleep. Miles was resting more and more, the morphine pulling him into a deeper slumber as his body began to let go. I fell into what I thought was a light sleep, but was deep in reality, and I was awakened by the sound of laughter.

I stumbled out of bed, down the hall, and into the bedroom where Miles's deathbed was set up. That's where I found Miles sitting a little more erect than usual, more alert than I'd ever seen him. Rashad was next to him, holding the remote he used to flip from one title to another, looking for music videos to watch together. Miles was singing along, his voice clear and strong, like I imagined it was before the illness took over. They were laughing, reminiscing, and for a moment, it was as if death wasn't in the room with us. It felt like the miracle Rashad asked for.

But I knew better.

What we were witnessing was what's known as the "death rally." It's a phenomenon that occurs sometimes just before someone dies, where they become more alert, more like their old self. It can be confusing and cruel, offering a glimmer of hope just before the end. I knew I had to tell Rashad.

I followed him into the kitchen when he went to get water. "Rashad," I said gently, my voice looking for places to hide. "What I'm going to say will break your heart." He turned to me, still smiling from the moment they'd just shared. The smile fell to his feet. I felt like I was about to shatter something fragile and precious. In all honesty, I was. But he needed to know.

I told him that what he was seeing in Miles is called a death rally. It's common for people to have a burst of energy or clarity before they die. I told him how desperately I wanted to wait until later to tell him that, after it was done, and perhaps while Miles was asleep, but now was the perfect time because it was his chance to ask him anything else he needed to know and get clear answers.

On Rashad's face was a deep, aching sadness. But he nodded, understanding. "I thought it was a miracle," he whispered, not wanting Miles to hear us.

"In a way, it is," I said. "You get to have a little more time with him, to say what you need to say." The night prior, Rashad said he missed the Miles who was there before the cancer most of all, and he feared he would never see him again. This was a gift.

Rashad nodded again and took a deep breath. When we went back to the room, Miles was still singing, his voice carrying through the house like an opera we'd been dying to hear.

Rashad sat beside him, took his hand, and asked the last question he had been holding on to.

"What am I going to do here without you?" His voice cracked, the words heavy with the fear and loneliness he'd been holding back. Miles reached up and cupped Rashad's face with a tenderness that broke my heart. "You're going to go on, Rashad. That's it."

I could see Rashad wanted more, wanted something tangible to hold on to, but those simple words were everything Miles could give and maybe they were enough. Maybe what Rashad needed wasn't an answer but to know that Miles was still there, still his.

Within the hour, Miles began to grow tired again, his voice fading as the pain in his liver flared up and the morphine pulled him back into the haze. Rashad held his hand, whispering to him softly, and I sat nearby, watching as Miles drifted away again, and with him, the vibrant energy of the death rally.

Miles died the next morning, with Rashad's head resting on his thighs and his eyes resting wearily on Miles's face. I found them like that, the room filled with a stillness that only comes when someone has left this world. I sat with Rashad, my hand on his back, offering silent support as we wept.

After a while, he pulled out his phone and played the recording from the day before. It was Miles's voice filling the room one last time. "You're going to go on, Rashad. That's it."

There was something beautiful in the simplicity of it,

something profound in its honesty. We don't always get the answers we're looking for, but sometimes we get what we need. Miles had given Rashad that gift, the assurance that he could survive this, that he would continue, even in the face of this unbearable loss.

We stayed there for a long time, listening to that recording, letting the words wash over us. And in that quiet room, I felt Rashad breathing deeply, attempting to fill a space that had just lost so much.

The death rally is a bittersweet moment that can catch even the most prepared off guard. It's that sudden surge of energy, clarity, or engagement that happens shortly before a person dies. When it occurs, as it did with Miles, it's easy to mistake it for recovery, for a miracle that's finally arrived. But recognizing it for what it truly is—a precious gift of lucidity in the final hours—allows you to make the most of that fleeting time. If you find yourself in a similar situation, as Rashad did, embrace the moment fully. Listen to their stories, ask the questions you've been too afraid to ask, and say what's in your heart. Don't waste time on what could have been or what might be—just be there, in the fullness of now, holding them close, sharing in their light, and loving them as fiercely as you can.

THE STRONG ONE

I'VE SEEN IT COUNTLESS TIMES. IN FAMILIES, WORKplaces, even among circles of friends—when death comes knocking, there's always someone who believes they must be "the strong one." Someone who takes it upon themselves to hold everything together, to make sure everyone else is okay while they themselves are quietly falling apart inside. Maybe it's you. Maybe you've heard people say, "You're so strong," and maybe you've felt the pressure to live up to that.

Let me say this: You don't have to. You don't have to be "the strong one." It's okay to fall apart. It's okay to feel every single piece of your grief, just like the folks you're maintaining the strength for. Not only is it okay but it's necessary—for your healing, for your soul, and for the well-being of everyone.

I've worked with many families who, following a death, fractured in ways that could have been prevented if only everyone felt safe enough to grieve together. It's a strange paradox, but in trying to be strong for others, we often end up making islands of ourselves, pulling further and further away—sometimes full of resentment. We miss out on the comfort, the closeness, the healing that can happen when we share our grief. So here, right now, today, I want to speak to you, the "strong one." Let's take off that weight together.

I was thirteen when my classmate Pam died. The news came over the intercom like an announcement about the lunch menu or a reminder about fire drills. A flat, disembodied voice: "If anyone needs to talk, the guidance counselor is available. Otherwise classes will continue as scheduled."

At first the room was silent, but then a ripple of whispers spread. The teacher cleared his throat, shifted awkwardly. Someone let out a sob. Someone else stifled a gasp. And me? I sat there, hands clasped in my lap, like I'd seen others in my family do when they lost friends.

I come from a family that prides itself on being "strong" in the face of death. Cry in private. Offer condolences, but don't make a scene. Hold yourself together so others have something steady to lean on. I had seen it in action over and over again, at funerals and hospital bedsides. Grief, in my family, was something you carried with discipline, not something you spilled into the open.

So when I walked out onto the field at recess, I was prepared to be the strong one. I gathered the friends who knew Pam best and we stood around the goalpost. I volunteered alongside hospice nurses, so I mimicked what I saw them do so many times before, when families came to see their newly dead relative: Talk. Speak the ache out loud. And for five minutes, I held my own grief back, nodding, listening, keeping my voice steady.

But then the stories started tumbling out—the way Pam sang, the inside jokes with her best friend, the way she could never open a juice box without spilling it, the way she wrote her name in bubble letters on every notebook she owned—and suddenly I wasn't holding it in anymore. The tears came fast and hot, and I didn't stop them. None of us did. We wept, we clung to each other, we let ourselves fall apart together.

Looking back, it feels almost strange that I was doing that at thirteen—leading a grief circle on a middle school playground. But it didn't feel strange then. It felt right. Because grief was not a thing to be swallowed whole. It was something to be held, to be seen, to be shared. In those moments, we weren't islands. We were a shore, rising and falling with the same tide, learning for the first time that being strong didn't mean standing alone.

First, let's acknowledge where this idea of being "the strong one" comes from. So many of us have been raised to believe that emotions, especially intense ones like grief, should be kept in check inside the house. Maybe you've been told that crying is a sign of weakness. Maybe in your family, vulnerability was seen as a burden. Maybe you feel that everyone has their own issues and you don't want to add to them. Or maybe, over time, you've developed this role because it feels like someone must keep things from completely falling apart when a loved one is dying, or when they've passed.

You are the one who arranges the funeral. You make sure the bills are paid, the meals are cooked, the kids are comforted, and everyone else's grief is managed. And while you're doing all this, you're swallowing your own emotions, stuffing them down for later. But let's be honest: Later rarely comes. And when it does, you're wondering why no one is available when you need to let those emotions show or when your grief has hardened into something heavy and permanent, sitting in the pit of your stomach, forgotten but ever-present.

You do this because you believe that if you fall apart, everything else will crumble, too. You convince yourself that your family needs you to be their rock, their anchor in the storm. But here's the truth: You're not an anchor. You're human. You have feelings that need to be felt, tears that need to be cried, and memories that need to be shared; and all these things should be done with people you love. Trying to hold all of that in, trying to be the one who never falters is not sustainable.

I remember a stretch of time when I suppressed my grief. I thought I was doing the right thing by bottling up my pain, by putting on a brave face, by being strong so that others could fall apart if they needed. But what I was actually doing was building a dam. And eventually watching that dam break.

Grief will always find its way out. Maybe it shows up as anger or resentment. Maybe it appears as depression, anxiety, or even physical illness. Grief is an energy, and energy, as we know, cannot be destroyed. It will demand to be felt in some form or another.

And here's the thing—the longer you wait to address your grief, the more tangled it becomes. It doesn't just go away because you ignore it. It festers. It settles into your bones. It becomes harder to talk about because the world has moved on, and you feel like you should, too. But you haven't. The grief is still there, quietly shaping the way you experience life, slowly disconnecting you from the people who love you.

I've sat with people who've held their grief for years, decades even. When they finally let it out, the pain is so deep and raw that it's like they're grieving all over again. The uncried tears, the unsaid goodbyes, the moments of anger or sadness that were never given space—they all come rushing to the surface. While that release can be healing, the damage that comes from waiting so long can't be ignored.

Holding in your grief doesn't make you stronger. It doesn't protect your family. It only deepens the pain and creates a disconnect between you and the people who are also hurting. When you pretend you're okay, you may be telling others that they should be, too. And that's a dangerous message to send because grief needs to be shared, not suppressed.

There is immense power in vulnerability. I know it sounds counterintuitive, but the more we allow ourselves to be vulnerable, the more we can connect with others, and the easier it becomes to move through our grief. When someone you love dies, the natural response is to feel. It's to cry, to scream, to mourn, to sit in silence, to be angry—it's all of it. And each of those emotions is necessary.

Grief is not neat. It's messy, it's chaotic, and it comes in waves of all sizes. Some days, you'll feel like you can handle it; other days, it will kick you to your knees. But the only way I've found to truly heal is to let myself feel everything as it comes. To honor my grief instead of running from it. To give my permission to be sad, to be angry, to be confused.

And here's the thing—when you allow yourself to feel your grief, you give permission to others to do the same. You become a model for what healthy grieving looks like. You show your family that it's okay to not be okay. That it's okay to fall apart for a little while. That it's okay to feel the full weight of the loss. In doing that, you create space for real healing to happen.

Now let's talk about the importance of grieving in community. One of the biggest misconceptions we have about grief is that it's something we have to go through alone. Grief is deeply personal, but it shouldn't be private. It's something that can, and should, be shared. When we grieve together, we find comfort in the fact that we're not alone in our pain. We connect through shared memories, through shared sorrow, through the shared experience of loss.

There's something deeply powerful about being in a room with people who loved the person you're grieving. When everyone is crying, when everyone is remembering, when everyone is hurting, there's a sense of togetherness that makes the grief a little more bearable. It's in these moments of collective grief that we find solace. It's here that we find the strength to keep going.

I've seen families transform through the act of grieving together. I know this will heal some of the broken relationships in my own family, I've watched as walls of silence and stoicism crumble, replaced by open, honest conversations about what the loss means to each person. In those conversations, in those shared tears, families begin to heal. They begin to understand that grief isn't something to be ashamed of. It's not something to hide or suppress. It's something that brings us together, that reminds us of the love we shared with the person we've lost.

Grieving in community means giving yourself the gift of support. You allow others to hold you when you can't hold yourself. In doing so, you create space for everyone to grieve in their own way, without judgment, without pressure to "move on."

So if you've found yourself "being strong for the others," I'm asking you to let it go. Let go of the idea that you must hold everything together. Let go of the belief that they need you to be their rock. Because the truth is, they need you to be human. They need you to feel, to grieve, to cry, to share your memories and your pain. They need you to show them that it's okay to fall apart sometimes, and that in falling apart, we actually come back together in ways that are more honest and more connected.

My advice to you, from the perspective of someone who has walked this road with many, is simple: You are allowed to grieve, and you don't have to carry the weight of everyone else's emotions on your shoulders. In fact, the best way to support your family during a loss is to be honest about your own emotions.

I remember Marla. She'd been the "strong one" in her family when her father died and when her little brother was murdered. "It's just who I am," she said. When her mother was dying, Marla stepped into her usual role, organizing everything, making sure her siblings were okay, and keeping herself busy so she didn't have to feel the full weight of what was happening. But as her mother reached the end of her life, Marla became more and more overwhelmed. Her body was tired, her mind was exhausted, and her heart was breaking, but she felt trapped in this role no one asked her to assume.

During one of our conversations, I asked her, "Who's holding you?" She stared at me for a moment before the tears came flowing. No one had ever asked her that before. She realized in that moment that she had spent her entire life holding everyone else together, but she had never allowed anyone to hold her.

Over the next few days, Marla slowly began to let go of her role. She cried in front of her siblings for the first time. She let herself express her fears and her sadness to whoever would listen. And something incredible happened. Her siblings stepped in to support her. They shared stories about their mother, laughed together, and cried together. For the first time in a long time, Marla wasn't carrying the weight alone.

After her mother passed, Marla told me that letting herself

grieve openly with her family was one of the best things she'd ever done.

If you take one piece of advice from me, let it be this: Don't deny yourself the experience of grieving. You don't have to hold it all in. Your grief deserves the same attention and care that you give to everyone else. It's through this openness, this vulnerability, that true healing begins.

LIAM

OUR CHILDREN, THE YOUNG ONES, UNDERSTAND MUCH more about life and death than we give them credit for. I think back often to Liam and just how well his mother Rasheda's exhaustion came through in that message she sent me on Facebook.

"How do I talk to my son about death?" she asked.

"Call me," I responded, sending my number almost immediately. I answered as soon as it vibrated and listened to a mother who had no road map for guiding her child through a life that, at eight years old, was already filled with great loss. The deaths of Liam's grandmother, his school friend, and now his uncle had left her questioning how to protect her son while honoring the realities of life.

"Should I even take him to the funeral?" she asked me. "What do I tell him about why this keeps happening?"

This is one of those conversations no parent wants to have, and yet it's one of the most important. Children like Liam don't need to be shielded from death; they need to be supported through it, with honesty and the same compassion we want for ourselves in the trying times. Death is a part of life, and though it comes in different forms—sudden, violent, expected—it's always an opportunity to help children develop their own understanding of it. What I shared with Liam's mother is what I've learned over the years as a death doula and as a father: Children deserve the truth, and they deserve it in a way that fits their world. It's not just about answering questions—they need space to grieve, express their confusion, and know they're not alone in this experience.

The temptation to shield children from the pain of death is powerful. I've seen it time and time again—parents telling little lies and half-truths, or avoiding the conversation altogether because they believe their child is too young to understand or that hearing the truth will cause unnecessary trauma. But the reality is, children like Liam are far more perceptive than we give them credit for. They sense loss even before they fully comprehend it, and what we leave unspoken often becomes more frightening than the truth. Kids, like adults, will allow their imaginations to run wild with anything that will fill in the gaps for them.

When Liam's grandmother died, his mother told him that she had gone to sleep and wouldn't wake up. While the sentiment was rooted in a desire to soften the blow as best she could, it only left Liam confused and anxious for more than a week about going to sleep himself. This is what happens when we sugarcoat death. It creates unnecessary fear and misunderstandings. Children are naturally curious, and they are more resilient when given clear, age-appropriate explanations about life's hardest truths.

When it comes to talking to children about death, honesty is not just about providing information; it's about creating a foundation of trust. In my experience, if a child senses that something is wrong, but no one is talking to them about it, fear shows its ugly head and anxiety straps in for the ride, all of which can be far more terrifying than reality. This is why it's crucial to have these conversations early and continue them throughout a child's life, making death a topic that doesn't feel taboo or shrouded in secrecy.

In Liam's case, his grandmother had been his favorite person, the one who showered him with love in a way that only grandmothers can. (Sidenote: Grandmothers are global treasures.) Her death was his first significant loss, and it rocked him at just seven years old. This would have been an important moment to talk to him about what death means. When children experience the death of someone close, it's a chance to start explaining the cycle of life in simple, concrete terms: "When someone dies, their body stops working. We can't see them, but we can still remember them and talk about them." For a child Liam's age, such an explanation can provide clarity without overwhelming them.

Children are constantly growing and evolving in their understanding of the world, so these conversations should evolve, too. What you might explain to a four-year-old will look different by the time they're eight. But the essence remains the same: Give them the truth in a way they can grasp, and let them ask questions.

When Liam's mother, Rasheda, reached out to me after the murder of Liam's uncle, I knew she was struggling with more than just her grief. She was wondering how much of this world she had to expose her son to. "He's already lost so much," she said. "I just don't want him to be scared all the time."

As a death doula, I was there to help Rasheda process her own grief while also guiding her on how to talk to her son in a way that honored his need for the truth.

I encouraged her to take Liam to the funeral if he expressed that he wanted to go. Funerals can be an important part of the grieving process for children, just as they are for adults. Funerals not only give children a chance to say goodbye, but they allow them to see the community of people who cared for the deceased, and to begin making sense of the loss. Of course, every child is different, and no one should be forced to attend if it feels too overwhelming. But Liam had expressed curiosity about his uncle's death and had already asked several questions about what had happened.

I suggested that before taking Liam to the funeral, she prepare him by explaining what he would see and hear. People would be sad and crying, there would be a casket, and his uncle's body would be there but that it was no longer his uncle—just the body he had lived in. I told her to let him know that it was okay to feel whatever emotions came up, and if he wanted to leave at any point, that would be okay, too.

Before a death comes around, children should already have some understanding of what death is. But when it's imminent or has just happened, the conversations need to be more direct. Clear language is important, as is avoiding euphemisms like "passed away" or "gone to sleep." Use the word "died" and explain what it means in terms they can understand, such as, "When someone dies, it means their body has stopped working, and they won't be coming back."

After a death, children need to be given the space to express their feelings without judgment or pressure to "move on." They deserve the same grace we should be giving adults after a death. Grief looks different for every child—some might ask endless questions, while others might seem uninterested. Liam's initial reaction to his uncle's death was anger, not sadness. He kept asking his mother, "Why do people keep dying?" That's the kind of question that doesn't have a simple answer, but it opens the door for a conversation about how life, death, and grief are all interconnected.

It's essential to remember that grief isn't a one-size-fits-all process for anyone, children included. In fact, one of the most helpful things you can do is to show children that grief is a natural part of life; it's something that we all go through, in our own way. Depending on the situation, it's okay to be sad, confused, angry, or even relieved. And it's okay to feel vulnerable. When adults hide their own grief, thinking they should shield their children from it, they miss a vital teaching opportunity. Sadness is not something to hide or be ashamed of.

In my experience, children benefit from seeing their parents express their emotions. Crying and talking about feelings openly normalizes the emotional process. It shows children that it's okay to feel deeply, even in a time of loss.

For parents like Rasheda, who want to help their children process loss but feel overwhelmed themselves, the key is simplicity and honesty. Rather than trying to protect children from the tough emotions or obscure truths about death, be straightforward but gentle. When Liam's mother sat with him the night before his uncle's funeral, she didn't sugarcoat things. She spoke to him honestly, telling him what he could expect at the service, without embellishment but with a soft understanding of his age and emotional state. She reminded him that it was okay to feel whatever he needed to feel, whether that meant crying, staying quiet, or even holding on to his anger. That in itself gave him permission to grieve in his own way, which is all any child really needs—space to feel, and the understanding that their feelings are valid, no matter how they appear.

So, as a parent or caregiver, it's okay to listen when the tough questions come. Even when you don't have all the answers, it's perfectly fine to say, "I don't know." But always reassure a child that they are safe and loved. And if you can, create little rituals or moments that help them honor their grief, whether that's through something formal, like attending a funeral, or more personal, like lighting a candle in remembrance. And remember that children, too, have their own rhythm in grieving. Some might want to talk about the person over and over, others may want to retreat. Your role is to meet them where they are, providing a sense of stability even in the midst of a difficult time.

The most important thing is to allow them to lead the way in their grief. Give them the space, give them the permission to feel without judgment, and above all, let them know that you're with them in whatever form their grief takes.

At the funeral, Liam was quiet but observant. He stayed close to his mother, watching as people wept and shared stories about his uncle. At one point, he tugged on her sleeve and asked if they could leave early. She didn't push him to stay or try to make him feel guilty for wanting to go. Instead, she nodded, and they slipped out, going for food. It wasn't an escape from grief but a moment to breathe, to come up for air in a sea of heavy emotions. Liam had been given the gift of choice—something so small yet so significant in a world where so much was out of his control.

In the weeks that followed, Liam began finding his own ways to honor the three people he had lost. He asked his mother if they could plant cucumber seeds in a bucket he found outside. His grandmother loved cucumber salads, and it would be his way to remember her. For his school friend, he hung a photo of the two of them on the wall of his bedroom, next to a drawing his friend's parents gave to Liam as a gift to remember his friend—a silent tribute to their friendship. And for his uncle, Liam decided to keep one of his uncle's old baseball gloves, which he used to teach Liam how to catch when he was on the T-ball team. Liam declared he'd use it when he got bigger and his hand could fit in it. These were simple acts, but they were his—his way of holding on, his way of understanding that the people he loved may be gone but they could still be part of his life.

THE WORLD DOESN'T STOP

THERE'S THIS MOMENT WHEN YOU'RE WORKING WITH someone at the end of their life, or a grieving family, sitting around a kitchen table, or in a hospital room, where everything feels suspended. Time itself warps. It's hard to believe there's an outside world when you're in that kind of space. The weight of sorrow is so thick, the conversations so heavy, it's easy to imagine that the rest of the world must be feeling it, too. But then you step outside—into sunlight or rain or a crisp breeze—and you see life continuing like nothing's happened. People are laughing at cafés, children are playing in parks, cars are honking, drivers are cursing, and the sounds of life are everywhere.

It's one of the strangest things about death, that feeling of disconnect between your inner world and the world outside. You've just experienced—or you are walking with someone who is experiencing—the profound, the heartbreaking, the unimaginable, and yet the world keeps spinning as if nothing is different. The sun rises and sets. The mail gets delivered.

Bills still show up. People still order their coffees, still go to work, still scroll through their phones.

In those moments, it can feel like you've been left behind. You wonder, "How could life just keep going like this? Doesn't the world know that someone in this house is dying? Doesn't it know that a life has ended? Shouldn't everything stop for a minute? Shouldn't there be a pause, even just a breath, for what is being lost or has been lost?"

I've never gotten used to that feeling. As a death doula, I've spent countless hours in rooms where death is looming or has just come. I've sat with families who are drowning in grief, and it always feels like the world should stop spinning, if only for a little while. But it doesn't. Life doesn't stop for death. It doesn't stop for grief. And that can feel incredibly cruel when you're in the thick of it.

For those who wonder how they'll ever step back into the world after their own world has come crashing down, I don't have an easy answer. The truth is, it's hard. It's disorienting. The grief doesn't go away, and the world doesn't wait for you to feel ready. But I can tell you this: You don't have to step back into the world all at once. You don't have to move at the pace the world seems to demand.

Give yourself permission to move slowly. You've just experienced something monumental, and it's okay if you're not ready to be "back to normal." The truth is, there is no going back to the way things were—to who you were. Not only because grief changes you and changes your relationship with the world but also because who you were before the loss was a person who hadn't experienced that loss. Being changed by grief is not a bad thing, though it can feel impossible in the beginning. The first time you step outside, it might feel like you're walking on a different planet. You might feel raw, exposed, unsure of how to interact with the world that has kept moving while you were standing still. Take your time. Ease into it. Take small steps. It might be something as simple as sitting outside for a few minutes, or going for a walk, or standing in line for coffee. You can wade back in, little by little, and find your footing in this new reality.

There's also something to be said for giving yourself permission to let the world go on without you for a little while. You don't have to keep up. You don't have to match the pace of life around you. If the world is going on like nothing's changed, let it. You can take a moment—or as many moments as you need—to sit with your grief, to feel it, to honor it. There's no rush to "get back" to life. Grief has its own timeline, and it's different for everyone. Don't let anyone, including yourself, rush you through it.

One of the hardest things about grief is the feeling of isolation, the sense that you're walking through a world that no longer looks or feels familiar. You may look at people laughing or living their lives and wonder how they can do that when the pain you're carrying barely gives you room to stretch. But the thing is, everyone carries grief. Everyone, at some point, has felt the world continue moving while they stood still. Though it may not feel like it now, there will come a day when you find yourself on the other side of that feeling. You will walk out into the world again, and it will feel strange, yes, but eventually it will feel manageable. And maybe one day it will feel okay.

I remember Annette, who stayed inside sitting with her husband during the last two weeks of his life. She didn't leave the house—not once—and when I arrived, at the request of her sister, I could feel the weight of the world shrinking for her, day by day. The living room became the entire universe—his labored breaths, the soft hum of the oxygen machine, the warmth of blankets pulled up to his chest. Everything revolved around that space, that time. The world outside became irrelevant, even unimaginable.

When her husband died, we sat together for hours, not saying much. It was as if time had stopped. For her, it had. But I knew that when she eventually stepped outside, the world would be spinning just the same, indifferent to her loss.

The next day, after we cleaned the apartment, I asked Annette to come walking with me. As soon as we stepped outside, it was jarring. The sun was shining, kids were laughing down the street, and cars zipped by like nothing had changed. But everything had changed for her. She froze on the porch, looking out at a world that hadn't paused for her pain.

"How can they just . . . go on? Don't they know what happened inside?" she asked, her voice barely above a whisper.

It's the cruelest part of death, I think—that the world doesn't stop. Annette hadn't been in a grocery store, taken a walk, or even heard the sound of passing cars for two weeks. She had forgotten that life keeps moving while we're standing still, swallowed by grief.

Annette stood there for a few more minutes. "You don't have to rejoin it all at once," I said, sensing her hesitation. "Let's just start with this trip around the block." And she did.

I don't mean to suggest that grief goes away or that you'll ever stop missing the person you've lost. But I do believe that, over time, you'll find a way to carry your grief with you into the world rather than letting it keep you from stepping out into it. You'll learn to live alongside it. You'll find moments of joy, even if they feel small or fleeting at first. And slowly you'll realize that the world may not have stopped for your grief but that doesn't mean the world doesn't care. It just means that life, in all its beauty and tragedy, is a cycle that continues with or without us.

Maybe that's the point. Life keeps going because it has to. Because even in the face of death, life persists. It's a reminder that there's still more to experience, more to feel, more to live for—even when it feels impossible. You don't have to rush back into the world, but know that when you're ready, it'll be there, waiting for you.

THE TRAIN

THE BIG METAL WHEELS OF TRAINS RIDING ON THE tracks soothe me more than the music I have on my travel playlists. This was the final leg of my trip that began with a flight from London Gatwick and would end at the Amtrak station on Main Street in Charlottesville, Virginia. Trains give me the opportunity to slow down and think about everything I can't and everything I avoid while I jet so fast and so far in the world, and I treat this mode of travel as a luxury. Honestly, any place that moves me to journal for more than ten minutes is a luxury.

I found a table in the dining car, settled into my seat, and noticed the woman across the aisle holding on to a napkin with a grip so tight that it seemed as though the fabric itself held the weight of the sorrow so visible in her red-rimmed eyes. She stared through the window, watching house after house pass by, and half smiled at a woman in her backyard, waving to us on the train as she pinned sheets to her clothesline. "How Virginia," I thought, and half smiled, too.

We quickly passed by the waving woman, and I watched the napkin in the passenger's hand crumple and twist beneath the silent force of her fingers as though it was her only lifeline.

I knew the look too well. The deep lines etched into her face, pulling her features into a mask she wouldn't recognize. The shadowed and hollowed eyes with heavy and swollen lids doing their best to cover and simultaneously stay clear of them. Her brows so close they looked as if they were knit together, and her lips, chapped and trembling, pressed into a thin, wavering line. Her sighs were silent, but her chest and shoulders moved loudly with every fleeting expression I could see in the reflection. When my friend Jennifer got married, she sent a list of acceptable colors to wear to the ceremony, and I chose taupe. The grayish brown would look beautiful against the Greek backdrop, I thought. But on this train, the gray that mixed into that brown woman's face was not beautiful; it was telling, and it was sad. She was traveling to say goodbye to someone who was dying, or she was traveling to pay her respects to someone who was dead.

Her phone rang every so often, an intrusion to the travelers sitting nearby who were unaware of what was happening. But for me, her ringing phone was information to help guide my actions. Before the phone rang, my first thought was to plop down in the seat across the table from her and extend a hand, but I try to never assume people want help, and she hadn't turned her face enough for me to see it in full but once.

I didn't want to embarrass her and make her think I came over out of pity or because she was being too loud.

The first call she answered in a voice barely above a whisper, and she murmured, "I'm almost there. Please tell him to hang on. Put him on." She forced a smile and spoke a little louder, repeating, "I'm almost there, okay? I'm almost home." She sat silent with the phone to her ear, but it didn't appear as though anyone was talking to her on the other end. After a few moments, the first person returned and she said once more, "Please tell him to hang on," and she hung up.

The napkin was no longer usable, and the tears looked as though they decided to wait for her to grab another before they fell. She stood, gave me her full face and a half smile, and made her way to the bathroom.

As the bathroom door clicked shut behind her, I leaned back in my seat and let my mind wander. What could I do? The weight of her grief was palpable, and I felt an overwhelming urge to offer some form of comfort. I thought about my own experiences, the countless times I'd sat with someone in their final moments, offering solace and a listening ear. What could I do in this confined space, on this moving train, to ease her pain?

An idea struck me. Reaching into my bag, I pulled out a receipt from one of my favorite London pizza shops and flipped it over to the blank side. With a pen in hand, I wrote a short note: "If you need someone to talk to, I'm here."

I folded the receipt and placed it on her table. It was a

small gesture, but having worked in grief and having grieved many losses, I know that sometimes the smallest gestures can mean the most.

She returned from the bathroom a few minutes later, her eyes slightly less red but still filled with a deep sadness. She saw the receipt almost immediately, likely wondering who scammed her into purchasing something, then unfolded it with a mixture of curiosity and caution. As she read, her eyes softened, and she first looked over at the men who were talking about finance and why Denver is a great place to live, then she looked at me. I gave her a reassuring smile, and after a moment's hesitation, she picked up her things and moved to sit across from me.

"Thank you," she said softly, her voice trembling.

We were approaching Culpeper, Virginia, according to the announcement.

"I don't even know where to start," she said.

"Is someone dying?" I asked.

She told me she got a call from her sisters early that morning that today was likely going to be the day their father died, and she was hoping to get to Charlottesville in time to hug him before it happened. We had fifty-six minutes left of our trip. Her face started to tighten and her hand was busy looking for something to grab to keep from shaking. I offered my hand to grab, and she took it.

I said, "Tell me your favorite memory of your father."

Her face softened a bit and she immediately gave me a full smile. And as she hopped from one memory to another, it softened even more.

From Culpeper to Charlottesville, we talked. She shared stories about her father, starting with her first memory of him; he was laughing when she caught him putting together the tricycle he'd gotten her for her birthday. "He was a terrific father of girls," she said, and I wanted to remember that line and turn it into a poem for her to always remind her of the man she was on her way to see, the man she hoped would hold on for at least a few minutes after she arrived at his bedside.

I offered her as much comfort as I could as a death doula, and in the fifty-six minutes we had together. I listened and offered words of understanding. As a grief advocate, I assured her that it was okay to cry no matter who was bothered by her tears. "If anyone on this train says something about you crying, we can fight them," I joked.

We laughed out loud for a few moments, and then there was a silence that allowed us both to explore our feelings and thoughts. She cried then, quietly at first, and then with more intensity, as if my words and the silence had given her permission to release. I reached across the table and held her hand, offering silent support as the train chugged along the tracks and the men now talking about Thomas Jefferson stared. In that moment, we were two strangers bound by the shared human experience of loss and the need for connection.

By the time we reached the station in Charlottesville, her tears had slowed, and there was a small but noticeable shift in her demeanor. She called her sister, who put the phone to her father's ear so she could tell him she was only a few minutes away. She hugged me tightly before we parted ways. As I watched her run toward the hospital, I felt that, in some small way, I had been able to help her carry her burden, if only for a little while.

I still think about her—a woman whose name I never learned—and her father, just as I think about the countless people we all encounter every day who carry heavy burdens of grief and loss—often without telling anyone or asking for proper help to carry them.

If you're wondering how you can help someone in a similar way, remember that it doesn't take grand gestures to make a difference. Writing a note, as I did, is one way to reach out, but there are many other ways to support someone who is grieving or in distress. First and foremost, it's about presence. Being present with someone, even if they're a stranger, can offer immense comfort. You don't have to know them or their story to hold space for their pain.

One thing you can do is simply listen. So often people need to talk, but they may feel that they don't have anyone who will truly hear them. Offering a nonjudgmental ear allows them to express themselves freely, and this can be one of the greatest gifts you can give. You don't need to have the "right" words to say. Sometimes it's enough just to be there and acknowledge their pain.

You can also offer physical comfort. A gentle touch, such as holding their hand, can ground someone in the moment, reminding them they're not alone. If physical comfort isn't appropriate, offering a quiet, compassionate presence can be just as powerful.

Sometimes holding space looks like helping folks in practical ways. If they're open to it, offer to run errands, help them organize tasks, or simply sit with them while they go about their day. I have many friends whose houses I'll drop in to be a warm body nearby when I know their grief is hitting them hard. Just being there while someone goes through the motions of life is an act of love. I think of one of my favorite films, and probably one of yours, too: *Steel Magnolias*. That scene after Shelby's funeral where M'Lynn breaks down in front of her friends, screaming, "I'm fine! I'm fine! I can jog all the way to Texas and back, but my daughter can't." Her pain is raw, uncontrollable, and impossible to fix, but her friends don't try to fix it. They don't tell her to stop crying or try to take away her anger. Instead, they sit with her in her anguish, letting her rage, letting her weep, letting her be. Their presence is solid, and it's what holds her up when grief is taking her down. *That's* what it means to hold space.

Ultimately, you don't need to know someone or understand their grief completely to offer support. Simply showing up, being present, and holding space for them—without expecting anything in return—can be enough to ease their burden. Compassion doesn't require a deep connection; it only requires an open heart.

CALVIN

CALVIN HAD A QUIET ENERGY, THE KIND YOU DON'T NOtice right away. You know the type—someone who has spent most of their life walking the line that's already been etched into the sidewalk and streets, doing everything by the book. It's often not until death comes tapping on their shoulder that they realize, "Maybe I should've been drawing my own line this whole time." Calvin had played it safe. Every move he made was calculated, every risk had very low stakes. It wasn't the life he truly wanted, but it was a life. His friend, a woman I'd traveled much of this world with and with whom I wound up in the strangest situations, told Calvin to call me shortly after his diagnosis and immediately after he told her he was ready to break out of that safe little box he'd built for himself. The little light shining through was his doctor telling him he likely had a couple of good years left to experience anything he hadn't already before the illness took over. Calvin's first words to me were, "I hear you can help me shake shit up." I had to laugh. He wasn't wrong.

By all accounts, my life has been one hell of a ride, so I'm certain that when the end comes, I'll wonder how I even made it that far, and I'll die laughing—maybe. I want that for everyone. People deserve more than a safe, predictable existence. They deserve to stretch their souls, to do something that makes their hearts race and their breath catch. So, yeah, I was more than happy that Calvin reached out.

His bags were already packed, his passport fresh from the mail, and his spirit practically vibrating with anticipation. He didn't need me to hold his hand. He needed me to hand him a map with all the spots marked "Wildness lives here." What he wanted from me was advice, and not just any advice. He asked me to take a couple of days and write down the things that brought me to my level of joy. I told him some of these things may be considered bad advice by some, and he chuckled, saying he wanted those most of all—the kind of suggestions that might make those who know him best say, "Wait, what?" But, according to Calvin, he wanted to be changed. He wanted advice that, if he followed it, would change his life, not keep him coasting on autopilot.

So, that's what I did. I went out and bought Calvin a journal bound in leather with crisp white pages and a leather rope to tie it shut. The kind of journal you find in a hundred years and wonder what explorer left it. Over the next couple of days, I sat down and filled the first few pages with what most would consider reckless and irresponsible advice, but advice that was real—advice that, in the end, might just be the best damn thing Calvin would ever follow.

The first thing I wrote in that journal, right at the top of the first page: "If someone offers you shrooms, take them."

I meant that literally and metaphorically. There's something about stepping outside your own head and seeing the world in a way you've never seen it before that shifts your entire understanding of what's possible. And sometimes that's what you need. Not just with shrooms but in life. It's the willingness to say yes to something that feels a little crazy, to open a door you'd usually keep closed. Calvin laughed when he read that first line, but I saw something behind his eyes—curiosity. That's what I was hoping for. Then he read the rest.

Don't make plans. Just go.

Spontaneity makes the organized people of the world break out into a cold sweat. Their hands get clammy, and their teeth start grinding. Calvin was the type to plan everything down to the minute. Every trip, every dinner, every detail of his life was planned in advance. Even his birthdays were planned two years out. That works for some people, but when you're at the end, what's the fun in knowing every turn before you get there? Calvin already had his first destination picked out—Oaxaca, Mexico. I told him from there, when he was ready to pack his bag, just pick a direction and go. Maybe it's Thailand for the beach, or maybe it's Paris for a walk along the river, where someone stops him and begs him to buy their sketch of a giraffe wearing a beret. Either way, it's going to be an adventure, and in my experience, the best adventures don't come from rigid schedules.

Get naked.

There's something freeing about stripping down—when it's legal and the mood is right—and remembering what your body feels like without all the armor. Since Calvin's first stop was Oaxaca, I told him about Zipolite, a kinda-hidden gem on the coast where nudity is absolutely welcomed. Getting naked is about more than just taking off your clothes. It's about shedding all the layers that society's put on you—the expectations, the rules, the fear of judgment—and just being. There's something about being naked in nature that reminds you that you're alive, that you're just another creature on this planet, wild and wonderful and completely untamed, if you let yourself be. Calvin grinned and promised to make his way down to Zipolite.

Call that person you haven't spoken to in years.

That one person you keep thinking about? We've all got someone like that. That person who meant the world to us once, but for some reason or another, we drifted apart. I told Calvin not to think about it too much. Just pick up the phone and dial the number. Maybe it's an old friend, maybe it's a sibling, maybe it's a lover from a lifetime ago. Don't think too much about what you'll say. The words will come. And if they don't? Just listening to their voice again may be enough. Enough time has passed. If someone mattered to you once, they probably still do.

Spend a whole day with no shoes.

Walking barefoot through the world sounds easy, but it's harder than it seems—especially when you start to notice how long it's been since you truly felt the earth beneath your feet. We spend so much time disconnected from nature, from our own bodies, that we forget what it feels like to be truly grounded. I told Calvin to find a quaint town, a forest, or even just a grassy park, and spend a day there, shoeless. It's a simple act, but there's power in it—power in reconnecting with something as basic as the dirt under your feet.

Eat the weird food.

Trying unfamiliar dishes isn't about being polite at dinner parties or pretending to enjoy a salad with a palmetto bug crawling through it. I'm talking about the stuff you'd normally wrinkle your nose at or pass on because it seems too strange. The world is full of flavors you've never tried, and I told Calvin to stop playing it safe. If you find yourself in Dubai, try the camel burger. If you're in Argentina, don't pass up the chance to eat sweetbreads if they're on the menu. Taste the world. Not just the food but the culture, the history, the people who made it. We don't realize how much of a place we miss when we stick to what's familiar. Calvin was mainly a burger man, and the weirdest thing he's ever eaten was okra. He was ready to give it a shot.

Tell people what you really think.

Politeness kept Calvin quiet for most of his life—holding back his opinions, smoothing things over, never quite saying what he really meant. But there's no time for that anymore, and I wrote it down for him in no uncertain terms: Tell people what you really think! Whether it's the person at the grocery store or your closest friend, be honest. Tell them how you feel and what you want. We spend too much time worrying about hurting feelings or causing waves, but at the end of the day, the truth is all we have. So give it freely.

If you want to get to the next place, hitchhike.

The idea of hitchhiking usually leads people to assume I've completely lost it. I know it sounds reckless, maybe even dangerous by today's standards, but I've done it countless times and for me, it's about trusting the road, trusting people, and letting go of control. You'll never know who might pick you up or where the journey might take you. It's a way of saying, "I'm ready for whatever comes next, and I don't need to control it." Calvin was the kind of man who liked control, who thrived on knowing what came next, so I knew this one would be a challenge for him. But that's the point. It's about letting go of the map and saying yes to the unknown.

If you love them, tell them. Even if it's "too early" or "too late."

Love, like death, doesn't care about your schedule—no matter how many rules we try to place around when it's okay to say it or show it. But the truth is, love, like death, doesn't care about your schedule. So I told Calvin that if he feels it, he should say it. Don't second-guess, don't hold back because you're afraid of rejection or because it doesn't fit neatly into some timeline. He nodded quietly when he read this one, a flicker of recognition passing over his face. I didn't push him. I just let him sit with it.

When you make it to a place that feels like home, stay longer than planned.

Life isn't a race, but we've been taught to treat it like one—always rushing to the next thing, the next person, the next destination. Calvin was goal-oriented, and once he met the goal, he moved on. But sometimes you find a place that wraps around you like a blanket knitted by your favorite grandmother, a place that feels like it's been waiting for you all along. When you get there—whether it's a small town, a hidden cabin in the Chattahoochee, or a city with ten million people—don't rush off. Let yourself linger. Stay a few more days. Maybe even a few months. If it feels right, it's because it is. You don't always have to keep moving forward. Sometimes the journey is about knowing when to stop and breathe.

Calvin spent the next few days reading and rereading those pages in his journal, turning the words over in his head, trying to reconcile them with the life he'd lived up until this point. He admitted he was scared but anxious. So much that his butt tickled, he said. Oddly, that's the same feeling I get when something great is about to happen. Nervousness means we're alive.

Calvin didn't need me to tell him to live the rest of his life cautiously, to keep doing what he'd always done. He needed me to remind him that life isn't just something you get through—it's something you grab with both hands and run with. Life is something that makes you sweat, bleed, cry, rejoice, scream and shimmy in the rain with a smile on your face. Life is not something we should attempt to make it through unscathed.

So, that's what I gave him.

Calvin and I left the same day. I returned home to the Chattahoochee National Forest, and Calvin made his way to Oaxaca. He was loose, relaxed, and open. I told him not to return until that journal was full of stories and his heart was full of life.

Many months passed. One day, Calvin called me up and told me he'd just been let out on the side of a road in Malaysia by a stranger, somewhere near a firefly farm, and he was waiting for a bite to eat. He said he couldn't read the menu and couldn't speak the language, so he pointed at a plate and hoped for the best. I told him I couldn't have been more proud. He laughed, and I could hear the freedom in his voice. He said he didn't know where he was going from there, but he didn't care. He just wanted to see where the road would take him.

And that's the thing, isn't it? We spend so much of our lives trying to control where we're headed, planning everything out, afraid of what might happen if we let go of the wheel for a minute. But sometimes the best thing we can do is throw away the map, stick our thumb out, and let life surprise us.

That was the last time Calvin and I spoke. He died a few years after. I hope whoever found that journal has it on a high shelf and pulls it down to read every so often. I hope they see him as the adventurer he was in the end and for the man he was before. And I hope that at the moment of death, Calvin looked back on those last couple of years of his life and saw that he lived.

That's all I ever wanted for him.

So to you who's been walking that same line drawn by someone else—a challenge: I want you to go out today, buy yourself a journal that makes you feel excited every time you open it. This isn't just a notebook; it's your permission slip to live fully, to lean into the life you've been too afraid to chase.

Open that journal and write down all the things you've

been putting off, the wild ideas you've brushed aside because they felt too risky, too impractical, or maybe just plain impossible. Write down the things that scare you, the things that make your heart race, the things that deep down you know you've been longing to do but haven't given yourself permission to.

Start with one. Maybe it's skydiving. Maybe it's telling someone you love them. Maybe it's packing a bag and booking that one-way flight to a place you've never been. Maybe it's something that sounds small on paper but feels huge in your chest. Whatever it is, it matters. Write it down. Stare at it. Let it make you a little uncomfortable. Let it make your butt tickle. Then I want you to make a plan to do it.

And don't just stop at one. Keep going. Fill that journal with the adventures you've been too afraid to chase, the moments you've been holding back from. Because here's the truth: The life you want is right there, waiting for you, but it's not going to come knocking. You must go after it. You must live it.

Calvin took the leap. He let go of the idea that life must be played by the rules. He allowed himself to embrace the unknown, to take the road perhaps best left behind, to feel that rush of being alive in the truest sense. And I want that for you, too.

Do it scared. While in college, I posted a sticky note on my wall with the following quote from John Greenleaf Whittier: "For all sad works of tongue and pen, the saddest are these, 'It might have been.'" With all my heart, I'm challenging you to live a life with few "It might have beens."

Go shake some shit up.

DOULA WITHOUT BORDERS

WHEN NORMAN CALLED ME TO BE HIS DEATH DOULA, I had no idea how much I'd end up learning. Not just about him but also about myself, about heritage and how deeply connected we are to the traditions that shape our views on life and death. Of course I knew death was a universal experience, something everyone will face sooner or later. Working with Norman opened my eyes to just how culturally rich the process of dying can be. Norman didn't just want to die peacefully; he wanted to die in a way that honored his Filipino Benguet heritage. I realized I wasn't just helping him die; I was helping him reconnect with a part of himself that he'd always carried but hadn't fully explored.

The Benguet, mountain-dwelling people in the Philippines, have rituals that connect the living with their ancestors, and Norman wanted to experience that connection as he approached the end of his life. He wanted to honor those who came before him, and in doing so, feel his death was part of something bigger than himself. It wasn't about fear. It wasn't about fighting death or running from it. It was about walking toward it as open as he could possibly be, knowing that the many who came before him, his mother included, would be nearby as he walked the path to join them.

Helping Norman navigate this journey sparked something inside of me. I realized I was in a kind of bubble, relying heavily on everything I learned from everyone I assisted and the things that came intuitively. This had never been a problem, but I wanted more. I was a collection of the people I helped die. If I wanted to truly serve people in their final days, I needed to understand where they were coming from, not just spiritually and emotionally but also culturally. The more I learned about the Benguet traditions and helped Norman incorporate those into his dying process, the more I wanted to step outside of what I've known, how I approached nearly everything in my life, and learn how other cultures made their journeys toward death. I wanted and needed to be a death doula without borders.

Norman's request was simple but powerful. He wanted his death to reflect his Filipino roots, specifically the Benguet traditions his mother shared with him, even though he hadn't fully embraced them in life. As Norman's death drew near, those traditions became something he was drawn to, something he needed to honor. So, together we found a way to bring those traditions into his home in a way that felt right for him. I did some research, and Norman reached out to his family in the Philippines—some he hadn't spoken to in decades—to reconnect and gather details. In the end, we kept it simple. We set up a small altar, what the Benguet people call an *atang,* in his room. The *atang* holds deep significance in the Benguet culture because it is a way to honor ancestors and invite their presence. The people offer food and other meaningful items to remember but also to create a spiritual bridge between the living and the dead, ensuring they remain part of the more important parts of life. For Norman, this became a sacred space where he could connect with his mother and ancestors and have them nearby when what he considered the most important thing he'd ever do happened. Don't we all want those we loved and who loved us to come back for us when it's time to go?

It wasn't just about the objects on the altar. It was about the stories, the memories, and the cultural ties that made Norman feel like he was part of something bigger. He found peace in knowing that his ancestors would guide him, and I found joy and purpose in helping him honor that connection.

Norman taught me that this work isn't just about guiding someone through the process of dying; it's about guiding them through the process of remembering who they are, where they come from, and how they want to leave this world. With Norman I realized that if I wanted to truly show up for people—all people who wanted and needed me to show up for them—then I needed to stretch myself even more. If it's true what the wise folks say and death happens to everyone everywhere, then I should be learning how people from all over the world view death—the traditions they hold close and the rituals that bring them peace.

After Norman passed, I became obsessed with understanding death through a global lens. I spent months reading and traveling around the world to understand end-of-life practices from different cultures, connecting with folks who honor the traditions for some deep diving. From Ghanaian traditions of elaborate, symbolic coffins to Mexican Día de los Muertos to Tibetan Buddhist practices, I explored it all.

Each connection added another layer to my understanding of death and how personal it truly is. It wasn't only about learning facts but also understanding the heart of each ritual and each practice. Being a death doula was never about only being there for the last breath. I want to help people create a death that reflected the life they lived, grounded in their beliefs and culture, if they chose. I want to be a bridge between worlds, a guide who can support anyone, no matter where they come from or what they believe in.

And then there was Marrakech.

One day, while traveling through Morocco with my son, I got the chance to put a little learning into practice in a way I didn't quite expect. We had spent the day biking through the desert—dust covering us, wind removing none of it. It was one of those perfectly long days of forgetting what day it was and forgetting the world aside from that location exists. But that world came crashing back when our driver, Youssef, who'd been quite talkative and entertaining, grew quiet as we passed a massive procession of men walking down the road toward what Youssef said was the graveyard. Thousands of men, moving as one, heading to a funeral.

Youssef's knuckles tightened around the steering wheel, and after a few long moments of silence, he finally spoke. "Would you mind if I stopped?"

Of course we didn't, understanding what was going on, and we asked, "Do you know who died?"

With tears, Youssef said, "My best friend who is like my brother died yesterday. They're burying him now."

My heart broke for Youssef. I hated that he had to ask for permission to attend his best friend's funeral, but I understood why he did. In Morocco, funerals happen fast—usually within twenty-four hours, in line with Islamic tradition. It's customary for the men of the community to come together and walk in the funeral procession. But here Youssef was caught between his job and his grief, asking permission to mourn his friend.

"Please, go," I said.

He nodded, pulling the car over as relief and sadness crossed his face. My son and I sat on the curb, watching as Youssef walked toward the crowd of men, disappearing into the sea of mourners. We couldn't help but feel helpless. Here was this man, grieving deeply but with no time or space to really process his feelings. In his culture, death was a communal experience, something that everyone participated in, but I wondered who was there for him in his grief?

In that moment I wished I could've done more for Youssef and for the thousands of men he walked with. He was grieving, yes, but who was there to ask him how he was really doing? I've come to learn—not only from research but also from closer work with clients from similar backgrounds—that in a culture where community support is so strong, the personal grief can sometimes be lost. Funerals are swift, collective, and respectful—but there's not always space for the individual to sit with their own pain and talk about their loss in a personal way.

A death doula could have helped Youssef in that moment—not necessarily to guide him through a long ritual or tradition but to offer him a quiet space to process. To ask him, "How are you feeling about this?" To give him permission not just to attend the funeral but to grieve in his own way, beyond the structure of tradition.

Had I been in a position to fully support him, I would have stayed with him after the funeral. I would've offered to sit and listen, to give him a chance to talk about the friend who was like his brother, to cry if he needed to, or even just to share memories. But Youssef needed to get back to work after dropping us off. Sometimes all someone needs is permission to feel their grief rather than pushing it down in the rush of tradition.

That moment in Marrakech reinforced everything I'd learned from Norman and my journey to be a doula without borders. Death is universal, but it's also deeply personal. Every culture has its own way of handling death—its own rituals, beliefs, and customs. My job as a death doula isn't just to know the right words or the right procedures. It's to understand where people are coming from, to help them navigate the end of life in a way that honors their culture and individual needs. That moment also reinforced for me that I will not always be able to step in as a death doula, but I can offer what I can in the moment. On the drive to drop us off, my son and I asked Youssef about his friend, holding space for the memories he shared.

Whether I'm working with someone who wants to honor their ancestors through Filipino Benguet rituals or standing by as a Moroccan man grieves in a sea of mourners, my role is the same: to offer support, to hold space, to be there for the living and the dying, no matter where they come from or what they believe.

Being a death doula without borders means knowing that death looks different from one corner to the other—and embracing that. It means learning about the wide variety of end-of-life practices, but more importantly, being present for each individual in a way that feels right to them. And in doing so, we ensure that no one faces death alone—whether they're surrounded by thousands of mourners or quietly passing away in their own home.

I REMEMBER ME

IMAGINE YOU'VE BEEN SHORT OF BREATH FOR A MONTH. Nothing too serious, just something that nags at you—something that can be explained by lack of fitness. Maybe you haven't been exercising enough, and that's why your legs ache, too. You probably pulled a muscle. But as the days stretch on and the heaviness in your chest gets worse with each stair, each walk to the kitchen, each breath, a voice in the back of your mind asks questions that feel inconvenient to answer.

I was twenty-two years old, fresh off the energy and ambition that comes with feeling invincible at that age, and I had a kid on the way. As it turned out, my invincibility had limits. What I thought was a simple need to hit the gym harder wasn't just my body giving me a nudge. It was a siren screaming out in ways I didn't want to hear.

When I was carried into the ER one evening by my pregnant girlfriend, Shauna, and my best friend, Cam, after falling to the ground in pain, I expected nothing more than a lecture on fitness from the doctors. Instead I was slapped with the kind of news that rearranges your entire sense of reality.

Sixteen blood clots—sixteen—starting from my ankle and winding their way up, with three finding their way into my lungs. I can still hear the doctor's voice, clear as day, when he walked toward my bed set up in the hallway because there were no rooms available in the ER, and told me, "You should have died a month ago."

A whole month, walking around unaware that I was living on borrowed time. I laughed, unable to do anything else at that moment. I can't even explain the surreal feeling of hearing that—of being told that every breath I took was one I shouldn't have had the privilege of breathing; that every step I took could have made it impossible for me to see the son who'd be born just one month later. Confused, shocked, scared, and only slightly breathing, I did the only thing I could think to do. I called my mom.

After all the tests, the family studies, the monthlong recovery that found me finally able to walk the night Shauna's water broke, the doctors found that I have a condition that can kill me at any moment. No warnings, no second chances.

The thing is, once you've lived with that knowledge—really let it settle in your bones—you see life a little differently. And here's the truth I've come to understand: Being alive and being aware that you're going to die are the same thing. Most people don't walk through life with that awareness right in front of them. They tuck it away, maybe letting it hover in the background, but they don't let it stare them down every day. Others pretend death will never show its face.

I don't have that luxury. To be honest, I don't think I ever wanted it.

Strangely enough, it's been a gift. A bizarre, terrifying, precious gift. When I was told I should have died, something in me woke up. Suddenly all the things that felt far off—the dreams, the adventures, the love, the laughter—they weren't far off at all. They were right in front of me, waiting to be lived. If I didn't reach out and grab them, they could disappear in an instant. Because I could disappear in an instant.

So, what did I do? I made a choice—a choice to live in a way that, if I were my own death doula client, I could look back and say, "Yes, this is exactly how you should be living." Freely.

My definition of freely living means really living—screaming, running chaotically through a forest naked, and dancing through the moments that most people don't even know they're letting pass by. I jump off cliffs into the ocean. I talk to strangers in line at the bus depot in countries I've been told I shouldn't visit, and hop on mopeds with them across borders. I taste life in all its wild, unpredictable flavors because I know—deeply know—how close death always is.

Each year, when I make it to see my hematologist, our meetings are short, sweet, and, yes, sometimes hilarious. She'll inevitably ask me, "So, what have you been up to this time?" And I'll smile and tell her the truth—whether it's strapping into a harness and jumping off a bridge in Ecuador or packing up for a last-minute road trip with someone whose name I barely know. And every time, she'll shake her head with a mix of disbelief and admiration as she scribbles down another year's worth of prescriptions for me to keep on hand. It's become our little tradition, an exchange of life updates against the backdrop of the condition I suspect will make another attempt on my life soon enough. And it will lose. I hope.

The thing is, my doctor isn't just shaking her head because I've been out there chasing adventure. She's shaking her head because she knows, better than most, that I have no guarantees. None of us do, really, but my awareness of that fact is front and center. Yet instead of being crushed by the weight of that, I've chosen to live. To really, truly live.

Let me be clear. Yes, sometimes it's about chasing the adrenaline. But more than anything, it's about finding joy in the ordinary and the extraordinary. It's about laughing with a stranger over bowls of soup on a Vietnamese street corner, sitting in silence on a mountaintop with someone you love, dancing in your living room just because the song playing is too good not to move to. It's about sipping coffee slowly, feeling the sun on your face, and remembering the tiny moments are all part of a much bigger picture.

I live for moments that make me say, "I hope I remember this when death comes."

I live with the reality of my own mortality, but I don't live in fear. Death, for me, isn't the enemy. It's a reminder. Every time I feel my chest tighten in the way that once sent me to the hospital, I remember I'm still here. That awareness has shaped me in ways I never expected, and I wouldn't trade it for anything. Because, yes, I could die at any moment—but so could you. The difference is, I live with that awareness every single day.

What do you do with that knowledge? What do you do when you know that death is as close as the next breath? You live. You live like it's the only thing that matters. Because it is.

You've been reading about the work I do, and maybe, without realizing it, you've seen glimpses of yourself in the stories—ways you've already done some of this before. So now I want you to really think: If you were your own death doula, what would you tell yourself about how to live? How would you advise yourself to spend your days, your hours, your minutes? Would you tell yourself to work more? To worry about all the things that may never come to pass? Or would you tell yourself to reach out, to love, to be present, to go and be in the world in a way that sets your soul on fire?

Talk to yourself right now. Listen to yourself right now. What do you need? How would you like to live?

Here's the truth I want you to sit with. You don't need a near-death experience to live like your life depends on it. I'm here to tell you that you have the permission to live fully—right now. Not when the timing is perfect, not when you feel like you've earned it, but now.

For me, every new breath is a second chance, and I've made it my mission to honor each one. I've found joy even in the presence of death. I've walked that tightrope of uncertainty, and it's made me realize that the secret to living well isn't about outrunning death—it's about dining with it. It's about letting the knowledge of your own impermanence remind you to be present, to love harder, to laugh louder, and to stop waiting for some magical moment when it feels like the right time to really start living.

Because, my friend, this is it. Right here. Right now.

I once wrote:

> I'd rather not die now. Not this autumn. It would inconvenience me greatly. There are so many other things I want to do. I have yet to stand at the helm of my destiny. I want to hitchhike from Paris to Monaco and stop along the way to eat a late dinner on a farm with happy lovers and fresh milk. I want to feel the thunder rising from the ground as twelve bulls scuttle by in Pamplona.
>
> I want to taste foods from Michelin-starred restaurants I can't afford: Restaurant le Meurice the next time I'm in Paris; Masa the next time I'm in New York with those friends who are never too busy. I want to know chefs by their first name and make cakes with laughing old women who never wrote down recipes. I want a loaf of good bread from a Spanish bakery to dip in oils from an Italian oil maker, and I want a bottle of good wine that isn't for dessert. Then I want four more. I want vodka with no chaser from a woman named Na-

tasha, and tequila with two worms—one for me and one for my drinking buddy.

I want summer's night and the coolness of a distressed hardwood floor on my toes, thighs, belly, and cheek. I want Deep South winters and the warmth of a lover pressed to me.

More Nina Simone covers by jazz bands on a stage in Montreal. I want to stand at the pinnacle and look over the edge and laugh as loud as I can for as long as I can at absolutely nothing. Stand ankle-deep in the Pacific with the sunshine slowly slumping into my beard, then my collarbone, then my bellybutton. Drift a canal. Stand in the Door of No Return in the House of Slaves. Run the wall. Climb the mountain. Find the bones of century-old lovers.

I want to sit on a train with my son and teach him the importance of writing letters. Most of all, I want to play with reckless abandon. Play like I played with my cousins when I was a boy. Barefoot at sunset, chasing lightning bugs through fences we were small enough to squeeze through, with my grandmother looking on, and me staring back believing everyone in this moment will never grow old or die.

So here's what I want you to do when this book ends. I want you to go outside. Feel the air on your skin. Take a deep breath and hold it, just for a second. Then let it out, slowly. As you do, I want you to remind yourself that that breath was a gift, one that you could've missed, but didn't. And now with that awareness, I want you to live. Really live.

Jump into the ocean, take the trip, call the friend, make the move, say the thing. Do it all—without waiting for the permission of some distant day in the future when it all feels safer. Because guess what? It never will be.

And that's the point. Life is messy and unpredictable and wild. But it's also beautiful and sweet and so, so worth it.

Afterword: They're Dead, Now What?

THE ROOM IS SILENT IN A WAY IT HASN'T BEEN FOR days—maybe even weeks. A different kind of silence than the one that filled the space when they were asleep or resting, staring out of the window, unsure of what to say or do, or just a bit fogged. It's a silence that doesn't breathe back. The air feels thicker, heavy with everything you've just lost. You've been bracing for this moment, but now that it's here, nothing makes sense. When his husband, Rowin, died, my dear friend Taj said, "It feels like I'm in this liminal time before I met him but after he lived." I've heard the same from others, like Maya, who just lost her mother. She told me, "It's like I'm living in a world that's both empty and full at the same time—she's gone, but I still feel like I should be picking up the phone to tell her about my day." That space between loss and memory is a strange one, where the past and present blur, and nothing feels real.

You're now wondering, "What do I do now? What's the first step? How do I start?"

First, take a breath. It might feel impossible, but do it anyway. The ground beneath you has shifted, and nothing feels steady. Grief is raw, disorienting. Whether this is your first loss or one of many, it doesn't get easier—it just gets different. But even in this haze, there are things that must be done.

Grief doesn't wait for you to find your footing. Your mind ricochets between the weight of absence and the demands of what comes next. The world doesn't pause, even when it feels like it should. There are calls to make, decisions you never wanted to face. But you don't have to figure it out alone. Below are the steps, and I will walk with you.

Confirm the death.

This is one of those moments where reality meets formality. If your loved one was under hospice care or passed in a hospital or care facility, you'll need to contact a medical professional to officially confirm the death. If they were at home without hospice care, call 9-1-1. Emergency responders will arrive, and depending on local laws, a coroner may also need to visit. I know it feels cold and clinical, but this is the first necessary step.

Hospice nurses are trained for this. If they are there or arrive soon after, they will help you manage the moment and handle the official paperwork for pronouncing the death. They will likely ask you questions about funeral home preferences and other immediate needs. If you haven't thought about these details yet, that's okay. Take a breath. You don't have to have every answer right now.

This is the moment where formality meets grief. Norman died at home, surrounded by loved ones. His after-death wishes had already been passed down to the little family he had, and they were sure they would get right to it with no problems once Norman was gone. But when the moment arrived, it was just too much to think about. It was still surreal. His hospice nurse—someone they had grown close to in his final days—happened to be there, and she confirmed his death, and the moment became real in a way that was both gentle and heartbreaking.

Notify those who need to be notified.

Once the death has been confirmed, it's time to notify the folks who should know. Those close friends, lovers, and supportive family members are watching their phones, hoping this call or text never comes, but it must. This isn't easy, and you don't have to do it right away, and you don't have to do it alone. If you have someone close by who can help make these calls, ask them for support. When my brother's girlfriend died, he called me, asking if I could make the calls because it'd only been five minutes since he got the word and knew it just wasn't going to be possible for him. Hearing yourself say out loud the words "They've died" can hit you in a new way, so be prepared for the wave of emotions that might follow. It's okay to cry. It's okay to pause. This is hard.

It's also worth knowing that some people won't know how to respond. You might get questions or comments you weren't prepared for, and they may not be comforting. People who didn't know death was near may ask, "Well, how'd they die?" Some may jump far ahead and immediately ask, "When's the funeral?" They're processing in the moment. People don't always know what to say in these moments, so they sometimes stumble. Be patient with yourself, and if you feel like it, be patient with them. If you don't have the energy to field those conversations, consider sending a text message or having a trusted person deliver the news for you.

When Kim's mom, Doylas, died, Kim was the one who had to call the family. She said it was one of the hardest things she ever had to do. It wasn't just about relaying the news. It was hearing herself say the words. It made everything feel more final, more real. And not everyone knew how to respond. Some people froze, then stuttered, trying to find what they felt were the right words. Some offered the same old clichés: "She's in a better place now" and "She's an angel now, looking over us." And some asked questions that made her feel even worse. But there were also those who immediately offered support.

Contact the funeral home, cremation service, or natural burial provider.

You'll need to make arrangements to transport the dead, and this is where you might feel the weight of the moment settling in. It's one of the more immediate tasks after a death, but take a breath. If you've already chosen a funeral home, cremation service, or natural burial provider, you're ahead of the game. If not, that's okay, too. One thing about death is that so many of us have experienced it, so we all know someone who knows someone who has the contact information for whoever you need.

If you're opting for a natural burial, there are providers who specialize in this, and they will guide you through every step, from death to burial. Whichever route you take, they will assist with transporting the body, scheduling services, and making arrangements however you need. This is where you must trust that the professionals will work with you to honor every wish in a way that feels true.

Secure the home.

It's important to make sure the property of the person who died is secure, especially if they lived alone. Lock the doors, close the windows, and set alarms if needed. This step is often overlooked in the initial shock of death, but it's a practical task that can save you from future worries. Understandably, there may be family and friends who want to enter to grab something that reminds them of the person who died. There will be a time for that. Now is not it. If they had pets, make arrangements for their care. If someone needs to stay at the home, it's good to have that figured out sooner rather than later.

When Luis's father died, nearly the entire family rushed to the house, each wanting to take something: his watch, a favorite sweater, even the half-finished crossword on the kitchen table. In the fog of grief, emotions ran high, and without a plan, things got messy fast. Luis had to step in, reminding everyone that there would be a time to sort through his father's belongings, but right now, the priority was securing the home. He bolted the door, documented what was inside, and made sure nothing was taken in haste. It wasn't about shutting people out—it was about protecting what was left until everyone could approach it with clarity.

Take care of the practicalities.

In the days that follow, there will be practical matters that need your attention. These tasks might seem daunting, but tackling them step by step will help you feel more grounded. Again, don't be afraid to ask for help. Often our friends and family and even people you barely knew will be standing by, ready to offer any support you may need.

Collect important documents. Locate the insurance policies, the will, and any prepaid post-death arrangements. If your loved one had specific instructions about their estate, now is the time to gather those.

Contact the Social Security Administration. If your loved one was receiving benefits, Social Security needs to be notified. In many cases, the people handling the body will do this for you, but it's important to double-check. If the dead had a spouse or dependents, they may be entitled to certain benefits, so be sure to inquire about those.

If they were still working, you'll need to inform their employer. Ask about any life insurance benefits or final paycheck details. They can guide you on what needs to happen next regarding their work responsibilities and finances.

Take a moment for yourself.

I want you to take this as seriously as I'm saying it: YOU NEED TO PAUSE. After you've taken care of the immediate logistics, give yourself permission to stop and just be. My friend and wellness partner Cara Chandler always reminds me to be a human *be*-ing after I've been doing way too much. I'm telling you the same. You've just experienced one of life's most profound losses, and that isn't something you can simply "handle" or "get through." Just be.

If you need to scream, scream. If you need to sit in silence, do that. If you need to go mad for a while, it's okay, and everyone dear to you will understand. Do it all in a safe space. There's no right or wrong way to process what you're going through. But I will say this: Don't forget to take care of yourself in the days ahead. Drink water. Eat. Moisturize, if you need to. Journal. Rest, even if sleep feels impossible.

Mourn.

The next few days will be filled with details about memorial services, burial or cremation, who gets what, and countless decisions that may feel overwhelming. Lean on those people who've told you "If you need anything, let me know." Don't hesitate to call those folks who asked "What can I do?" Let them know you're hungry, that you need paper plates from the store, that you just want to hear someone else breathing at the other end of the couch. Whatever it is, if people offer to help, let them. When good, genuine people want to pour love onto you, let them. You don't have to carry all of this on your own.

There's no right way to mourn. Some people dive into the planning process as a way to stay busy, while others feel paralyzed by grief and unable to move forward. However you're feeling, it's valid. These streets you're navigating now are new. Even if you've lost someone before and know the weight of grief, you've never lost this person. Every step you take is part of your journey.

Handle financial and legal matters.

At some point you'll need to address the financial and legal aspects. This can feel like too much to deal with so soon, and it can also feel so slight when you're still processing the loss, but it is all very important and necessary. Don't hesitate to ask for help from a lawyer or financial advisor, if you need it.

Here's a breakdown to help you begin:

Obtain multiple copies of the death certificate. You'll need these for everything from closing bank accounts to claiming life insurance benefits.

Settle the estate. If your loved one had a will, the executor will manage this process. If there's no will, the estate will go through probate, and a court will determine how assets are distributed.

Close accounts. This includes bank accounts, credit cards, utilities, and subscriptions. This is where having multiple copies of the death certificate will come in handy, as many companies will require it.

Contact insurance companies. This includes life insurance, health insurance, and any policies related to the dead's home or vehicle. Once you let them know about the death, they'll guide you through the claims process.

Plan the memorial service.

You may be one of the lucky folks who was given very specific instructions on how the memorial service should go—who'd sing, the size of the limo, the color of the flowers, and what bar should host it. But if you're like my cousin and was told by your dying person, "Do whatever you want," then this is the time to reflect on what would honor them best. Or do nothing. If you decide to do something, it could be a traditional service, a celebration of life, or something entirely unique to their personality and preferences. And it doesn't have to be right away. Don't rush. This is a deeply personal process, and you're allowed to create something that feels meaningful to you and those who loved them.

Lean into your grief.

This is going to sound counterintuitive, and not that you haven't been doing it throughout the last many steps, but let yourself feel it. Some days you'll feel like grief is eating you, gnawing slowly and loudly, starting at your fingernails, ending at your heart. Other days it'll feel like a quiet ache. However it shows up, lean into it.

Find ways to honor the dead in the days and weeks ahead and know that grief doesn't go away, but it changes shape. It evolves as you learn to live with the absence of the person you lost.

Seek support.

As a mental health advocate, I let all people all the time know to not be afraid to seek support. Whether it's through friends, family, a therapist, a grief counselor, or a support group, you don't have to go at this alone. Grief, like your heart at the beginning of this, is heavy, and it's okay to ask for help carrying it. There's no shame in feeling lost by it all.

None of this will feel easy, and that's because it isn't. Death rearranges the world as you knew it, and grief demands more from you than you ever thought you could give. But you're here, still breathing, still moving, still figuring out what comes next. That's enough for now. So when it all feels like too much, when the weight of absence presses in, when you don't know what to do—just take the next small step. And then the next. You're not alone in this. Grief is a road walked by many before you and many still to come, but today, right now, it's yours. Keep going.

Acknowledgments

TO ACKNOWLEDGE A LIFE—ITS WEIGHT, ITS PRESENCE, its absence—is to give it shape beyond memory. This book is, in many ways, a collection of those shapes. It exists because of love, loss, and the spaces in between, where I have been held and where I have learned to hold others. It exists because of the lives that have intersected with mine: the ones I was born into, the ones I walked toward, the ones that found me unexpectedly. Some of those lives have ended, some are still unfolding, and some continue on in the spaces we can't always name. But all of them shaped the way I move through this world.

My story begins with the one who first held me, the one who shaped the edges of my world before I even knew how to name it. **Doreen Wells,** my mother, whose hands are firm when they need to be, gentle when it matters most. Whose voice carries wisdom, warmth, and the unspoken lesson that love is not just given—it is shown, again and again and many agains after. And **Larry Wells,** a father who's as steady as the ground beneath me. There, always, in ways that didn't ask for recognition. A foundation I didn't always know I was standing on but one I could return to, without question, whenever I needed.

Dennis Karl Brown Jr., my brother, the one I have walked through hell with—not once, but twice. We are still here. That alone is something to honor.

Somewhere along the way, I learned what it meant to be a companion in grief, to sit beside someone in the wreckage of loss and not try to fix, not try to explain; just to be. **Kim Turner** reminded me of that. She let me walk with her through the raw, unfiltered edges of sorrow, let me see it up close, let me ask, "What does it feel like?" And she answered, honestly. That kind of trust is not given lightly.

There are roots in me that were planted long before I knew how to tend to them. **Jacqueline Anthony**, my godmother, made sure I grew up with pride deep enough to hold me steady. **Grandma Katie Walker** reminded me that family is not a word you use—it's a thing you show up for, in the quiet moments, in the hardest ones, in the spaces where no one is keeping score. Sometimes with complaints, but always with love.

And then there was **Grandad George Walker Jr.**, who let me be there when it mattered. Who let me teach him that vulnerability is not weakness. That to be seen fully—especially at the end—is its own kind of strength. I looked at him and thought, "This is exactly who I'll be, if I'm given the gift of a deathbed." And **Grandma Geraldine Walker**, who held the love that shaped him, who gave me the space to see him clearly.

Some people give you a second family without ever making a grand gesture about it. **Michele Holmes** did that when she shared her mother with me, when she gave me a place to belong. **Delphine Sharpe** did it when she let me love her through her dying. Not everyone allows that kind of intimacy at the end. She did.

There were brothers in the bonds I chose. Eron Riley, Bobby Marshall, Jamail Sills, and the rest of the **Gamma Theta Chapter of Kappa Alpha Psi Fraternity.** These men who showed me how to carry each other, how to lift without asking for anything in return.

And there were places, too, that shaped me. **Esalen Institute** opened a door I didn't know I needed to walk through, showed me I was more than just a bridge; I was also the one crossing it.

Christopher Stahling, you reminded me that our stories are worth telling, even the ones we aren't sure anyone wants to hear. Thank you for listening to mine, for giving me a place to rest my head when the railroad Toni Morrison talks about was also an option.

There is something to be said about time. About having it, about losing it, about making the most of what's left. **Perry Jones,** my father, I am glad we have had the chance to know and love each other as men. **Glenna Stinnie,** you took care of me in ways that will always mean something.

Some goodbyes come too soon. **Debbie Lee Yingst,** you were there when I first stepped onto this path with purpose. You were a part of the reason I stayed on it. I wish I had told you that. I wish I told you "Thank you."

Maryrose Simmons poured love into me when the world was too much. **Sheena Burnside** held up the mirror and showed me who I was—then taught me how to protect that person.

And then there is my son, **Darnell Walker-Jones.** The love of my life. I wasn't sure I would be here long enough to know you as a man, but I am. And you are even more magnificent than I ever imagined.

Lane Clarke, this book would not exist without you. **Angela Guzman,** you made this collaboration feel easy, made me feel understood from day one. You took the chance. You saw the value in this work. Thank you.

To my family—the Walkers, the Joneses, the Wells, the Anthonys, blood and beyond.

To those who have trusted me to help them die as close to the way they wanted as possible. To the families who let me stand beside them in their grief, who allowed me to bear witness to their love, their pain, their resilience. Your stories live in these pages, too.

And to those who saw something in me before I could see it in myself. **The teachers, the mentors, the librarians.** The ones who handed me books instead of punishments, who let me question everything, who understood that misbehavior was often just curiosity with nowhere to go. Who saw past the trouble to the light inside.

Irene Elizabeth Jones. The one who showed me that this is not work. This is just what we do when people need us.

To the living, to the dead, to those somewhere in between: I see you. I carry you. Thank you.

About the Author

DARNELL LAMONT WALKER is a death doula, Emmy-nominated children's television writer, producer, and explorer. Born in Charlottesville, Virginia, he creates spaces worldwide for healing through storytelling, end-of-life care, and workshops on grief, resilience, unlocking the writer within, and radical empathy. He joyfully lives in the Chattahoochee National Forest of North Georgia.